When everyone else seems to be exploring their own navels or has just figured out that "language" doesn't "mean" "anything", Bialer takes our hand and pulls us outward into a much larger, stranger world. Bialer is a successful street photographer and painter and he brings his artist's eye to these amazing poems, showing us the unspectacular real world behind the supernatural. These are poems that celebrate imagination and folly and the heartbreak that is being human and trying to make sense of a world that is infinitely bigger than even the craziest of us imagines. UFOS, The Bermuda Triangle, alternate universes, estranged families and wonder all swirl together in these expansive, totally original poems. I read a lot of poems and I never have come across anything quite as beautifully strange as Bialer's.

—*Matthew Rohrer*
Author of RISE UP and DESTROYER AND PRESERVER

Matt Bialer's original, compelling, entertaining poems spin and split and carry on in a somewhere space that bristles with familiar facts and strange possibilities. Kinetically poised between anecdote and fable, between sci-fi invention and historical record, between technological information and the wildest imaginings of paranormality, these energetic, observant, humorous, heartfelt and thought-packed poems strike their own notes of staccato narrative, bringing to immediate life a multitude of idiosyncratic, bizarrely inhabited worlds. Bialer's winningly intimate, hyper-aware voices orchestrate a serio-comic cohabitation of ordinary people with Charlie Chan, Bozo the Clown, Houdini, the *X-files*, the crazy-time universe of *Lost*, the case studies of Oliver Sacks, Pynchon paranoiacs, Dracula movies, and hosts more. His strobe-lit collage narratives fold us into their odd, often comic entanglements with no fussy explanatory apparatus, so the weirdly inexplicable becomes "part of our everyday living." As, I guess, it should be.

—*Eamon Grennan*
Author of MATTER OF FACT and STILL LIFE WITH WATERFALL

TELL THEM WHAT I SAW

TELL THEM WHAT I SAW

POEMS BY

MATT BIALER

TELL THEM WHAT I SAW

Published in January 2014 by Stanza Press, a division of
PS Publishing Ltd. All rights reserved. The right of Matt Bialer
to be identified as Author of this Work has been asserted by him
in accordance with the Copyright, Designs and Patents Act 1988.

"Synthetic", "The Ice Road", "Calls", "Ghosts" and "The Thing in
the Basement" first appeared in *The Green Mountains Review*. "AntiChrist"
first appeared in *Retort Magazine*. "Philip K. Dick Head" first appeared in
Forklift, Ohio. "Spear of Destiny", "Conference Room", "Crop Circles",
"VR" and "Silence" first appeared in *Le Zaporogue*. "Knowledge" and
"Storm Chasers" first appeared in *H_NGM_N 11* "Twins first" appeared
in *BLIP*. "The Land of the Lost" first appeared in *Catch Up*. "Tell Them
What I Saw" and "Past Life" first appeared in *Cultural Weekly*.

ISBN 978-1-848636-98-9

Design & Layout by Michael Smith
Printed and bound in England by T.J. International

Stanza Press
Grosvenor House
1 New Road
Hornsea, HU18 1PG
England

editor@pspublishing.co.uk
www.pspublishing.co.uk

CONTENTS

ACKNOWLEDGMENTS

I want to thank Kris Saknussemm and Jennifer O'Grady for their incredible help with these poems. I could not have done this without you guys. You expected a lot and I thank you! Thank you!

Another big thank you to my friend Seb Doubinsky for all of his support. You are a true punker.

I also want to give a big thank you to my friend Matthew Rohrer for his support and cheering me on. Rock on!

I want to thank my lovely wife Lenora Lapidus for inspiration and support. I want to thank my precious daughter Izzy for listening and teaching me.

I also want to thank Elisabeth Frost, Jim Nisbet, Lynn Hightower, Kelsey Osgood, Nancy Jean Burns, Jenny Breukelaar, Adam Chambers, Traci Slatton, Robert Whitehill, Dave Appelbaum, Dan Mandel, Sharon Guskin ,Eamon Grennan, Stewart O'Nan, Paula Bernstein, Sheila Williams, Susan Skolnick, Alice Twombly, Celina Osuna, Suzanne Wise, Elizabeth Twiddy and Ole Wesenberg Nielsen. Thanks for reading closely and supporting.

Thanks to Irving and Thelma Bialer and Roni, David, Mary and Michael.

And—finally—a big thanks to Brentley Frazier, Elizabeth Powell, Matt Hart, Nate Pritts, Alexis Fancher, Michael Smith, Matthew Revert, Pete and Nicky Crowther.

WATCHING
"THE AMAZING SPIDERMAN"
UPSIDE DOWN

One of the most vivid memories of my American 60s child-hood is watching the Spiderman cartoons upside down on the couch. I distinctly remember the grainy black and white image, the tinny voices and the thrill of being (a little) scared. Sometimes I wore a blue spaceman helmet, with a light on top—but then I'd be sitting down. In the late sixties that I remember, everything had to do with space as a kid. There was the Space Needle, the space cookies, the latex astronauts, the plastic spaceships... We were surrounded by space—and we loved it. Yet, we could understand that there was more to life than the azure and mysterious planets—we also caught glimpses of other images behind our parents' backs who thought we would be sleeping by then—wounded soldiers being carried by their comrades, beautiful explosions in the jungle, black people marching with their fists raised, strange looking people with long hair playing music, and so on. We lived in an in-between world of technological magic and incomprehensible violence, then late 60s colors and style giving the whole a certain "cachet," albeit a weird one.

When I first read Matt Bialer's poetry, those images jumped back into my mind. It felt as if I had tuned in a forgotten, yet essential, channel of our past. Of what had made us and this country morph the way we had. I recognized the UFOs, the shining chrome planes, the dark weirdness of the unsaid shared only through knowing eyes... It was an extraordinary moment of warmth and anguish (in the good sense) all rolled into one.

For Matt Bialer's poems deal exactly about that: the truth behind the unbelievable, the shift of certainties, the limits and breakthroughs of technology—all of it going, mostly, terribly wrong. But they are also poems where the weirdo is right, the monster sensitive and the rational scientist a bastard. They tackle "truth" and "belief" in a radical way, blurring the conventional zones affected to each, focusing more on the result of the confrontation than on choosing sides. In that way, Matt Bialer is an heir of the best of American poetry—namely Whitman, for the modernity, William Carlos Williams, for the close to the bone style, and Carl Sandburg, for the humanity.

The latter being, for me, the most important—after all, styles and genres pass with the wind and a good summer rain. But what will prevail in these poems is the profound exploration of the psyche, the careful respect for the protagonists' situations, the moving reflections on identity and conformity. Matt Bialer isn't just "telling stories in a poetical way"—he is, deep down, a true, merciless and accomplished poet, in the noblest sense of the term. His verses vibrate, his rhythms function and his constructions are amazing. But form here is at the service of a greater good—to attack what we call "reality" and "rationality." In these times of "bad squareness," as they would have said in the 60s, it is truly reminding us what poetry is all about. And they makes me want to watch those "Amazing Spiderman" episodes, once again, upside own.

—*Sébastien Doubinsky*

TELL THEM WHAT I SAW

For Lenora and Izzy—You are my world

MANY WORLDS

1. THE THEORY

He never speaks
To his son or daughter
Always wears black suit and tie
At the dinner table
His uniform
Constantly puffing Kents with a filter
Vodka martinis
Swept back black hair, glasses
Mustache/goatee—strokes
Lost in thought
Reviewing a hand, poker night
His strategic analysis cronies
Scribbling lines of computer code

As a boy, his son always hears—
Though not from him
That he's some sort of hot shot physicist
Or was
Before he was born—early flare out
9 years old, the son is banging his drums
Doorbell rings, split level house
The father answers
Siamese cat bolts
Young wide eyed grad student, red hair
I'm looking for Mr. Everett

I am He
I found your dissertation Sir
THE THEORY OF UNIVERSAL WAVE FUNCTION

It blew my mind

Relative State Formulation
The Many Worlds Interpretation

1943, twelve years old
Hugh Everett III writes Albert Einstein
Is it something random
Or unifying
That holds the universe together?

Dear Hugh, there is no such thing like an irresistible force
And an immovable body

Spring 1955, Niels Bohr, Founding Father
Quantum Mechanics
Delivers lecture at Princeton University
Doesn't complete his sentences
Hugh, a graduate student, snoozes
In a photograph, outside Proctor Hall,
Beneath stained glass window
68 year old Danish Nobel Laureate
Surrounded by four students
All wear black academic gowns
Hugh laughs, thin, eagle profile
Cigarette in hand
That night a group of students
After a slosh or two of sherry
With Bohr's assistant
Steer discussion to paradoxes
Of Quantum Mechanics, ridiculous things
Hugh—tipsy, offers conceptual scheme
Inconsistencies, so-called paradoxes
Removed

6

Schrödinger's Cat—
In the sealed box
The flask is shattered
Releases the poison that kills the cat
Or not
The cat simultaneously alive and dead
Until the viewer looks inside the box
Not so for Hugh
The cat has split
Both alive and dead
Different universes
As the wave function evolves
Through time
It constantly splits off
New universe for each coordinate point

There is no collapse

Sits at this desk in his room
Graduate College
Sharpened pencils, yellow legal pad
Bottle of Cherry Herring
Manual: How to Write a Dissertation
Chain smokes, plays poker and ping pong:
Student friends—Competitive at everything
137 pages
Typed up by his future wife Nancy
His advisor John Wheeler
Begs him to delete the word
"Split"
Back and forth negotiations, revising
Wheeler likes Hugh but conflicting loyalties
Hugh's degree put on hold
Bohr and his circle vehemently reject the theory

Bohr: *Wave functions do not make sense outside of*
          viewing
          Experimental results

Everett writes   *NONSENSE!*

Spring 1959
Hugh and his wife and baby girl
Fly to Copenhagen
Will sit down with Bohr
Personally sell him the idea
That undermines all of Bohr's

Stay at luxurious Hotel D'Angleterre
Hugh goes for walks
While he waits for meeting
Canals
Long dark lakes
With gulls, ducks and swans
Likes to snap pictures
With his new toy:
Microfilm spy camera—
Buildings, lakes, trees, kitty cats
Visits the famous Little Mermaid statue
Which sits on a rock in the Harbor
The head of the statue

Recently sawn off by vandals
A new head is produced
And placed on the statue

Sits in a café
Under the influence of
Many glasses of Carlsberg Beer
Excitedly scribbles an equation on napkin
Discovers what will become
The Generalized Lagrange Method
For Solving Problems of Optimum Allocation of Resources
Or more simply known as
The Everett Algorithm

Dinner with Bohr
His palatial home
Built by Founder of Carlsberg Brewery
Donated its use to the Danish National Treasure:
Niels Bohr

Next to the Brewery
Stinks of fermenting hops and stale beer
Hugh likes the smell
Salmon first course
Main dish of pork roast
Hugh pulls out a cigarette
But politely told in Denmark
Do not smoke at the table
He refrains but with great effort
After dinner
Bohr difficult to understand
Looks down, thinks deeply
Half way through sentence
Gets up, walks to the blackboard
To relight his pipe
Which only stays lit for a few sentences
And then Bohr repeats and repeats
Polite listening
A lot of mumbling

It's a no-sale

Cannot understand why
A perfectly logical idea
Has so little impact

It's all in the math
It's in the math

II. THE MAN IN THE BLACK SUIT

January 2, 1971, two US marshals
Accompany a White House courier
Dulles Airport to LA
Important classified package
For President Richard Milhous Nixon
His San Clemente residence
The flight delayed, east coast storms
The courier and his bodyguards
Indulge in some drinks, the Admirals Club
Down the bar
A pudgy, goateed man
Wearing a black suit
Drinks shot after shot Beefeaters gin
Chain smoking Kents: long, tapered plastic filter
Overhears their conversation
He knows who and what they are
During the flight
The fat, goateed man
Relishes several more drinks
Gets up to go to the can
When he returns
He suddenly pulls out
A miniature spy camera
From a small case attached to his belt
Snaps a picture of one of the marshals
Chewing on the in-flight chicken lunch
Pissed off
Why did you do that?
Alcohol and cigarettes on his breath
The man replies *For my files*
The marshal proceeds to the cockpit
Radios for the FBI to meet the plane
But there's no time

Man disappears in the crowd
Later, authorities raid the Holiday Inn

Near Santa Barbara
Room of Dr. Hugh Everett III
President of Lambda Corporation, Arlington VA
Computer modules for the Department of Defense
Attending conference on Advanced Techniques
Data Processing
Affected by several drinks
Merely stupid act I did on spur of the moment
In his luggage the FBI agents find
Two brand new Super 8 films
Pussy N Boots and **Persian Sex Kittens**
And an odd scrap of paper
With suspicious calculus equations
Scrawled on top: **IMPROVEMENT ON ONTOLOGICAL PROOF AGAINST THE EXISTENCE OF GOD**
Inside his spy camera
Besides the image of the air marshal
Chewing his in-flight rubber chicken
Pictures of trees, houses
Ripples in a duck pond, felines
Most astonishing to the agents
Inebriated man
Has an incredibly high national security clearance
Q clearance
Access to some of the Pentagon's most precious secrets
Software he designed
For targeting major cities
Throughout the communist world:
Nuclear Armageddon

III. MAKING THE WORLD SAFER, AT LEAST THIS ONE

First works for the Weapons Systems Evaluation Group, Department of Defense
Then founds successful software company
Lambda
Exclusive to the Pentagon

11

Algorithms and mathematical calculation
Different scenarios

Complete nuclear war
Between the US and USSR
First strike or retaliation
Some destroy both countries
Many lead to win for the US
Simulations involve destroying China too
Trade offs between
Deploying specific weapons systems
As a function of kill ratios
3423 Hydrogen bombs
Vaporize more than 1000 targets
285 million people, USSR and Eastern Europe
Megadeath
Reduced sunlight for years
Massive amounts of black smoke
And aerosol particles
From the fires in to the upper troposphere

Hugh usually drinks
Three perfect Jack Daniel Manhattans
With lunch
Always craves fine food
A prime rib, filet mignon
Returns to the office
Takes a nap
Arises refreshed
Breath reeks of alcohol
He now has a son
But he constantly tells Nancy
The kids are her project
She defers to Hugh as usual, always very quiet
Likes to watch science shows on PBS
Both lenient parents
Sometimes the daughter stays out all night
Brings home strung out guys,

Some much older than she
The son always banging his drums, loud electronics
In and out of rock bands
Hugh doesn't mind
Hugh doesn't notice

Every Friday afternoon at the office
Sherry hour
Once a month a pot luck square dance dinner
Likes to flirt with the women
And poker night
Evolved from the WSEG Poker Group
Hugh plays hard
Strokes his beard
Reviewing his hand
Beach condo, St. Thomas
US Virgin Islands
Sometimes takes a long weekend
With a secretary from the office
Wading in the water
Cigarette in his mouth
Looking up at the cloudless sky
Shields his eyes from the sun
Pictures with his spy camera
Not of her
But of waves breaking
Repeatedly breaking
Over his pale legs

IV. A COME BACK, OF SORTS

August 1977
Hugh is tickled
Invitation from the University of Texas, Austin
Give seminar on
His Many Worlds Interpretation
First time anyone
Has paid attention in years

Packs Nancy and the two kids
Second hand Cadillac Seville
Drive from Virginia to motel

University Hall packed
Curious students and professors
An exception to the School's no smoking policy
Made for Everett
Wears his rumpled black suit
Pocked with cigarette burns
Explains basics of the theory
Answering questions
Staccato voice
Paces back and forth
Chain smoking, gesticulating

With every event that
Could happen in more ways than one
Universes branch off
In different directions
Moment to moment
We divide in to multiple versions of ourselves
Alternate realities
A world where dinosaurs survive
The Nazis win World War II
Snow in the summer
Nuclear winters
And so on

V. END OF DAYS

Their home reeks of cigarettes
Newspapers and magazines
Stacked all over
Fallout shelter in the basement
Hugh's teletype
Directly connects to the Pentagon
Bottles with batch numbers

Bad homemade red wine
And his new toy—
A CB radio
His handle: Mad Scientist
Regularly chats with redneck trucker friends
Occasionally invites them over
Beers and barbeque
Strokes the cats
More Kents, his long curled fingernails

Evening of July 18, 1982
Nancy and the daughter
Both out of town
The son is washing dishes
Hugh chats pleasantly with him
About music and poker
One of the few conversations
They ever have
As the son leaves to go out
Notices his father
Lying on the opposite side
Of his usual position on the coach

Watching late night news
Seems odd but is late to meet friends
The next morning the house feels too quiet
Finds his father's lifeless body in bed
Wearing his white shirt and tie
Feeling his cold and heavy body
The son realizes
That this is first time
That he has ever touched his father

VI. THE LAST REQUEST

His father did not believe in God
There will be no funeral

He will be cremated
Then as per his father's instructions
His remains will be thrown in the garbage
Nancy keeps the urn
In a grey filing cabinet in the basement for two years
Then one day, out of nowhere,
She abides by her husband's request

VII. RECORDINGS

Thirty years later
The son is the only one left
He is now a famous rock musician
Stage name of "E"
More known than his father ever was
Writes a song about
Finding his sister
Unconscious on the bathroom floor
Rushes her to hospital
Returns home later that night
His father looks up from his newspaper
Taps ashes in to tray on his chest
I didn't know she was that sad

In the basement
E finds boxes of used airplane tickets
Cancelled checks to liquor stores
Stained hotel receipts
Super 8 porn films
Thousands of sheets, yellow legal paper
Covered in Algorithms

Then he finds a tiny Panasonic Dictaphone
The type that spies use
Only known tape recording of his father
The son drums in the background
A cocktail party

How getting sloshed on sherry
Helped him come up with the equation
Yes, *that* equation
Another tape, 60 minutes long,
Just of a cat purring

VIII. MANY WORLDS

Imagines he's a boy
In a park with his father
Climbing over his big hairy chest
The air is clear
His father smells of aftershave
White musk
He is looking up at the tall oak trees
Everything bright, high contrast
Shields both of their eyes
From the two suns
Hums a tune
Not just a different time
It was a different world
What's that Daddy?
A song I wrote
I'll teach it to you

At E's live show
Lights go low
When you Wish Upon a Star plays
A black coffin-like box rolls out
Studded with blue and red jewels
Blinking lights

Against a powder blue backdrop
E pops out from the box
Fitted white jumpsuit
Do rag, sunglasses, shaggy brown beard
Chomps on a fat cigar

Strums his baby blue electric guitar
Harsh voice but fragile
Sings *Beautiful Freak*,
I am the Messiah
Novocaine for the Soul

One night during the tour
The big black box rolls out
Empty

RESTRAINT

Big shop day   They just finished renovations   Grand reopening
Aisles over a mile long   Daycare   Kids can watch the sea
monster   Ours stay with us
    Follow the arrows   Grab the usual eggs in bulk, paper
towels, canned emu, gull thighs   I worry about getting lost
Not enough restraint   Tastings
Foot long scorpion stings, saber-toothed crustaceans, shark
bellies   We move past the wax figures   Life-size casts
of your family in minutes
    I know one that did   Then they disappeared
Just the figures were found   Ghosts good ones and bad   For
your home   There's one in ours   A bad one   Malcontent
from years ago   Finally the UFO sightings   Guarantee of at
least one   Or the pricier Abductions   But not on this shop
Our cart is full
    I scratch at the strange implant in my neck   Imagine
the living room   Where they came upon the wax figures
As if they were going to rise for dinner

SEA HAG

I have been travelling for years   Even switching continents
Sleeping Under overpasses   Abandoned piers   Sitting alone at
an occasional café   I arrive at a city that is slowly falling into
the sea   When I spot you at the fish market   Among the stalls
of Dungeness crab   I never thought I'd see you again
You look straight at me   Undulating, tentacled anemone
An explosion of poisonous cells   Terrified I flee   Duck into an
old cannery   Stink of fish and sweat in the floorboards   I stay
there all night   Only a boy   Those hundreds of years ago
When you discovered me   Delicate and fernlike   You took me
down   Past the brown and blue-green algaes   Threadlike red
seaweeds   Fronds and irregular sheets   Free floating kelp
I wake up to a boardwalk   On the ocean   I don't know what
year I'm in   Grottos, canals   Ferris wheels, Arcades, saltwater
taffy, scream machines, shooting stars   A carriage
To the Giant Sea Serpent's Lair   In the funhouse mirrors I see a
tired old man   I sit down in a sideshow tent   Watch the sword
swallower, a contortionist, Insectavoras   And then I see the
tanks   A little one with trapped nymphs, Naiads, tapping at the
glass   My hands are wrinkled and webbed   And then I see you
Chained in the largest tank   A three headed Hydra pleading to me
Daughter of Poseidon   Goddess of the Drowned   You can
swallow oceans

CLAIRVOYANCE

After my bridge game
I'm washing dishes
Sipping chamomile tea
My daughter on the phone
Mom, Sam's been telling me
Who will be calling
Or dropping by before it happens

Could be a coincidence dear

Predicts fire drills in school
Selects correct color M & M candy
Hidden in my hand, every time

Mom, he's like Grandpa

Oh, we don't know that

I want to get him tested

I don't think you should

II.

1931, Duke University
Parapsychology Lab

Experiments in telepathy,
Clairvoyance, precognition

Dr. JB Rhine, once a botanist
Begins the study
Develops parapsychology
Into a branch of science
Abnormal psychology
Coins the term ESP: Extra Sensory Perception

My father, test subject
Lab's first star
Zener card test
Guesses more cards correctly
Than anyone before

Working class kid from New Jersey
Economics undergrad student
Knickerbockers, fedora hat, maroon & orange thin striped tie
A volunteer

About the size of regular playing cards
Decks of 25
Each card one of five symbols:
A cross, star, wavy line, circle, square
Chance is 20% correct

First long test
300 card series
Dad averages 49% correct
Accurately guesses 9 cards in a row
Odds: one in two million
Three days before finals—
700 runs through deck
41% accuracy rating
Guessed from campus library cubicle
100 yards from where Professor Rhine sits

Reshuffles cards
Slips in occasional blank one
To fool Dad but can't

Beautiful Spring morning
Rhine takes him for relaxing drive
Plymouth Roadster, rumble seats
Blue Jay Point County Park
Light up, pack of Luckies
Idling engine
Correctly guesses 15 cards in a row
21 out of 25
Probability: one in 30 billion

Just as the Professor is convinced Dad is true clairvoyant
His ability disappears

III.

I'm online
Chat Room
Senior dating service
Anybody, anywhere
My daughter—instant message—
Wants to bring Sam over
A dream he had about me

We're at the kitchen table
Sam's in the living room
Playing with his Game Boy
She knits to relax—
A scarf of the Queen of Hearts

He keeps a journal of his Psi experience
Knows what kids are saying about him
Across the school yard—
He's too short, too hyper, a tattle tale

In his book bag
The Invisible Man by HG Wells
The body does not absorb
Or refract light

His dreams—exact photographic glimpses
Grandma, you were younger, long brown hair
Years before Grandpa
Fall night, raining
You're sobbing
A white car speeds away

IV.

After one spectacular year
Dad never scored so well again
Extremely exhausted
Feels rushed—boredom, distraction
I could do better if I took my time
It still hurts
Drops out of Duke
The Depression   Can't afford it

His ESP part of our everyday living

My birthday party—sock hop
Bubble gum pink poodle skirts
Dad, dressed as Clarabelle the Clown
Baggy striped costume
Correctly calls a quarter
Being flipped 17 times in a row
Predicts all of his friends babies—
Date of birth, exact time and weight

We all knew he was IT.

Sometimes the police
Show up at our door
Heavy duty black and white cars
Dad steps out on to the gabled porch with them
Plaid sports jacket, flapped patch pockets
I know a local girl's been missing
Summer night: crickets, cigarette smoke,
Muted voices
Dad comes back in—doesn't say a word

Shares his precognitive ability
With my friends in college
Writes and tells them
Dates and times of future events
Quotes exact license plates
Someone they'll date next week

One night in college
I'm in my sorority
Dad phones
Tells me he had a vivid dream
A young man, he loves me,
White Mercury Comet, green interior

Daddy, I haven't met this person yet

In the dream, stormy weather,
I'm distraught   Car drives off
He can't read the license plate

V.

The Mall
Café outside Toys R Us
Sam's inside
Spending all of his allowance
My daughter, keeps stirring her coffee
He sees people who are not there

Telepathic about his birthday presents
School shrink says he's hyperkinetic
I grab her arm
Keep him grounded in love
Don't treat his gift as strange or abnormal
Sam runs out, excited, his new games—
Pokemon for the Wii, Computer Solitaire
Grandma, I had another dream about you—
You're young, leaning against a wall
Miniskirt, big hat, florals
The same man, arms around you
Moppy hair, black turtleneck
Talking and laughing

Keep him grounded in love
Don't treat his gift as strange or abnormal

VI.

First meet him at the Halo Lounge
Tikki décor, perfect martinis
Out with my girlfriends—
Windowpane stockings
Exotic music
Ramsey Lewis' The In Crowd
He graduated two years before
Lives off campus
Singles apartment complex
A painter—Pop Art
Camel cigarette packs, Esso gas pumps
Bartends to pay the bills

Never been with a man before
Poker nights—My first royal flush
Frenzied dancing—The Electric Circus

Groove to Howlin' Wolf, the Youngbloods
Café au Go Go, The Gaslight

Teaches me beatnik poetry
Smoke grass, sex, good whiskey

I want to bring him home
Introduce him to my family
Will you come?
Sure   Then I'll take you down to mine

VII.

Dad later develops Alzheimer's
Does not seem to suffer
Except in the early years
Watches his memory fail
Sad to see someone he's known whole life
But cannot come up with a name

One day I'm visiting
Place photos from his youth
Memory Box
So he'll recognize his room
One of him and his brothers—
Little boys, shaven heads, smiles
Face full of mud

We're in the Communal Area
Play Gin Rummy
He turns a card face up
Tells me too bad that boy left

      Daddy, I was in college

Says you aren't Catholic

Yes, that's what he said

Tried to find him years later
Concentrate, concentrate
All I got was a blank card

GLOBSTERS

They can't be identified   Washed up on beaches
Blubber detached from bones   Featureless whitish masses
Russians found one on the Sakhalin shore
Not a fish   Not a crocodile or octopus
Skin with hair   Eel shaped sharks, sea serpents with beaklike
snouts or two tusks at the extremity of the lower jaw
Fibrous muscle tissue, membrane, white coats, mantis heads
Some like enormous broken hands   The Stronsay Beast
Tecoluta Sea Monster   Carcasses in Prah Sands
Cancelled life forms washing up on shores all over the world
Even here in Brooklyn   The Navy Yards
I see one tonight stagger out of the river   A monstrous thing
Alive Covered with brown hair   Its head like a horse with tusks
and flippers   It groans and beckons me to come
I run all the way home   Out of breath everything seems normal
again   I see nothing on the late news   When I'm half asleep
I believe I'm being snared in underwater nets tearing at corpuscles
and thews   The next morning I scan the paper   No new sightings
I imagine diving to tremendous depths   Past distant lights
A long lost sunken city   As I lie here on the examining table
waiting on the doctor's word

THE LAND OF THE LOST

I.

Dive off tree house
On to leaf piles
Jim's underwear shows, always does
His clothing's unwashed

> *Avoid dangerous Sleestak at all cost*
> *Ancient race,*
>   *10 foot tall Reptile Men*
> *With crossbows*
>   *Gurgling sounds*
> *Like the murky fish tank*
>   *in Jim's basement*

> *Duck in to a Pylon*
>   *Dimensional portal—metallic obelisk*
>   *Larger inside than out*
> *Matrix table studded with grid:*
>   *Colored crystals that we shuffle—*
>   *Summon electrical storms*

Afterwards, Oreo cookies and milk
Take for ourselves   His mom's hospitalized
Anxiety attacks   Stopped conversing
Jim—Mets cap over oily brown hair,
Galaxy Diner tee shirt—

30

Dunks and licks the moons out of middle
Tap on the fish tank
Neon tetras darting back and forth
Their eyes are prisms
Touch the parchment
Of his Dad's constellation charts
Navigator during the War
B-29 Superfortress
Me, I love fighter planes
Give me Hellcats, Wildcats, Mustangs

    Bet you an SR-71 rescues us from the Land of the Lost
    A supersonic plane can't jump dimensions
    Speaking of that, let's go to Hawk Rock
    No, it's getting too dark

II.

Monkey bikes fly through the woods
Near Route 301

    Dive-bombing ships, bridges

Dark sky, no moon
But we know the way

By stone chambers
No one knows who made them
My Dad says they're old root cellars
Jay says Druids thousands of years ago

        There were never Druids here Jay
        What about the UFOs
        What UFOs

Approach chamber everyone calls
Mother Earth
Or Womb

Oval in shape, slightly underground
Slab roofed

Faint red glow
       Coming from the inside
A hum like an electrical generator
       Vibration
Do you hear that?
Drastic change in temperature
       Freezing

Jay enters the chamber
       I wouldn't Jay! Shit!

I enter too
Noise stops
       No red
       All dark inside
Feel like someone watching

Force slams both of us

       Knocked down, dirt floor
       Look for who did it
No one there

What the fuck?

Slowly get up
Knocked down again
       Unseen force

Stay down
       Figure of very tall man
       White robe

Eyes glow yellow

       Looks at us

Then gone

Get up, run outside
Cloud of mist

White light
Very bright on hill

Like it's in the air
Illuminating the trees

Whitish blue
Like a spotlight

Moves up and down
Across

Sky distorted like heat waves off tar road
We run

III.

Nearby, business trip
First time in more than a decade
Sell large private jets
Fortune 500 companies
NETJETS *BE THERE*
Rival trying to steal our client
My boss: *You're in a fishbowl*

Have a morning to visit Jay
Took over his parents house
Single, never married
Discovery film crew
With him in the basement
Diagrams of stone chambers
Photos of saucers, amphibious alien heads

Middle grade science teacher
Paranormal Investigator
Mets cap over balding head
Red M.I.T. tee shirt
The Multiverse, String Theory
Beings From Other Dimensions

They could be lost
Can't get back
They could be observing us

The crew going back to Hawk Rock
Jay and a group, camp there
Wants me to come
Speak on camera, our experience
I won't

Just people fooling us Jay

Back in my hotel room
Call my wife and daughter
I miss them
Half nod out

Running in the dark
With the lights,
Air shimmering
I see more of them

Swimming
In the distance, robes
Hooded figures
Their eyes are crescents

We're in a fishbowl

SURVEILLIANCE

Men in jumper suits break in to my house
Force a metal mask over my face
A baboon head riddled with lights and raw circuitry
Can't breathe   My eyes sting   I hear animal wails
Now I am constantly under surveillance
For a crime I didn't yet commit
Two dark SUVs parked in front
Monitors, headsets, infrared, chips
I wish I knew what terrible thing I will perpetrate
Maybe I can help   On TV I see they are making arrests
Sleeper cells, murderers   Sweeps through office buildings
Frogmen in the river searching for evidence
Implants in my head sample, image, probe
Looking for the exact moment the plot will hatch
I try to think of only agreeable things   The zoo
With my wife and daughter   Behind the cage
Spider monkeys with armbands   Jumping in the trees, grooming
I sit alone at an empty outdoor café   Government vehicles follow
I remember the Probocis monkeys in the mangrove swamp
Swimming with their infants on their hips   My daughter pointing,
    laughing
Tonight I dream a troop of Howler monkeys fashion deadly spears
From sticks   Peeling back the bark   Sharpening the ends
Their faces half-amphibian   I can hear the sirens

WHITE SPACE

He finishes three crossword puzzles a day
Sometimes more
Working through a list of clues
In strict order
Filling in white squares with letters
Forming words or phrases
As if he'll remember who he is
Or what he's doing
Meet Henry—
Most studied patient
In the history of brain science
1953, when only 27 years old,
Experimental brain surgery
To ease severe, chronic seizures
Surgeon removes two finger shaped slivers of tissue
Including his hippocampus
The seizures stop
But Henry hasn't formed a new memory
In 55 years

My girlfriend swings by
Both postdoc   She's in the Computation Lab
Combinations of mathematical modeling,
Simulations, behavioral trials
Dimples—loose, braided blond hair
Much smarter than I
                    Do you know what day it is today?
           December 13th?
                    Yes   It's also our 3rd anniversary Stupid!

36

Uh-oh
You're in deep shit
I'll take you out
Try to kiss her   She pulls away
Damn right you are
Bends down to the wheelchair
Henry, it's going to snow later
They should get you home
Yes, he replies
Quiet, always polite, soft spoken
Over 100 scientists have interviewed, tested him
In all Neuroscience textbooks
But no memory of this
Puzzle books in a basket
Attached to his chair
Shaky hand pencils in, erases
Crossword grids, 180 degree rotational symmetry
Pattern appears the same
If the book turned upside down
Helps him remember words, his childhood

She asks Henry
Do you know who I am?
I believe I do yes
Didn't we go to high school together?
No declarative memories
Those concerning people, places, facts after 1953
Nixon Presidency, Gulf War
The rise of Starbucks, Amazon
All came and went
No accessible trace
Except for the occasional surprise
If you walk away longer than 20 seconds
You are erased
My girlfriend just did
5, 4, 3, 2, 1 . . . . . She is no longer
Comes back
Henry, do you know who I am?

37

His lips quiver
          Yes, I think so
          Didn't we roller skate together?
We've heard this story before
Over and over
Believes she was with him sixty years ago
Saturday afternoons of laughter
Pompoms, colored lights, popcorn, limbo music
Black carpet with Day-Glo designs
Eating huge pickles with her at the end bench
Whoosh!   Winning the Shoot the Duck competition
We hear about his banjo lessons
Classmates in school
Going up in a small airplane over Hartford
The address of his house: 63 Crescent Drive
His .22 caliber pistol
Target practice in the woods with his big brother

They'll take him home to his niece
Now his guardian
Could never live independently
No friends
For years, lived with his parents
Daily routine: The Safeway
With his mother
Glass arched marina shaped façade
Carrying the groceries back to the Chevy
Counts the parking lot striped lines
Mowing and raking the lawn
Watching television
Looking at newspapers and magazines:
Boy's Life, Collier's Special Issue—Space Travel Pictures
Then later the crossword puzzles
White cells connected in one mass
Through shared sides
To form a single polyomino

As promised, I take her out for dinner

Even though it's snowing hard
Our favorite: Legal Seafood
Chowder and lobster tails
Debate false memories, introspection, illusion
Then to the mall for a movie
Pan's Labyrinth
At the end, the sadistic Captain Vidayl
Leaves the labyrinth
Hands Mercedes the baby
Requests that they tell his son
Exact time he died just as his father did
Mercedes refuses
Your son will never know your name
Her brother shoots him in the face
Henry stuns us sometimes
Remembers that Archie Bunker
Calls his son-in-law Meathead
Accurately draws a floor plan,
The house he lived in, after surgery
Small, only one floor
Kind of learning that takes place
Very slowly, hour after hour
Finds his way from the living room,
To the kitchen, in to his bedroom
Before he left today
Tapped the side of his head with his fist
Knock on wood

Afterwards, intense snow
Vast parking lot
Bundled up, our arms locked together
Walk against bitter wind
Slip and tumble, laughing
Holding hands, eyes squint
Snow everywhere—
Try to find the way to my car
Gusts blowing us, whiteout

GHOSTS

My doctor checks for ghosts again
I step in to the frosted tube in his office
Fills with light, thick vapor And we see them
Swirl around me   Orbs   Groping mouths, grunts, whispers
Screams from behind a thick wall   I wonder
If they are related to me   "No, they're mongos" the doctor says
Not really any one   No ethnicity or time period
Just bitter afterlife   Certain people attract them
Residual energy from a prior event   The tube
Fills with purple gas   I know this will get rid of them
OFF for spirits   The doctor once told me we don't know
Where they go   "Probably find someone else"
And then I go home feeling much lighter
Later, as I sit in the living room of my old house
I imagine being the last remaining one An apparition
In someone's peripheral vision   Earthbound
Footsteps forever down the same hall

REMOTE VIEWER

Wazirstan   A concrete bunker
I float through the walls   Up one floor
An unconscious man tied to a chair
Head down, long brown hair, beard
He seems far away, blurred   I describe
All detail to my monitor who records me
From an altered state of consciousness
I target coordinates using latitude, longitude
Remote in space and time   Strategic missile forces,
Political leaders—theirs and ours, research
And development facilities   In Jakutia
Winds and snowstorms   Some sort of installation
Is making them nervous   Satellite reveals cranes
Rapid construction   I travel the extensive
Underground tunnels   View Scud missles
Biological, chemical warfare labs   I find my targets
In the mind of the collective unconscious   Detect
And decode visual and sensory data   There are
Eight of us   We eat in the cafeteria by ourselves
Failed marriages   We don't exist   Project Sunstreak
The Soviets, Chinese, Czechs had one   We couldn't
Fall behind   I was a third generation highly
Decorated officer   Elite Airborne Ranger Company Commander
Training exercises in Jordan   I was accidentally shot
In the helmet   Nightmares, graveyards, golems beseeching me
I was afraid they'd find out   Then the classified file
Read it overnight   Let's talk   Now my wife's left me
I totaled our car on the magnolia tree   Bruises, cuts
Found roaming a strip mall   I tell my son we've witnessed

Vast alien architecture   Black skies   Towers
In amonia clouds   And we all saw the afterlife   The only
Thing it could've been   Shrouds carrying bundles   Not
Noticing us   My son a special operations infantry man
Just got engaged   He doesn't want anyone to know
About me   The doomed Pan Am flight   Moments
Before detonation   Everything is murky   Again
I am walking up the aisle   Looking for the overhead bin
With the brown briefcase   A little boy with sandy hair
Wants his mom to rub his back   He always does

THREE JESUSES

I am waiting for Jesus Christ
To enter the room
Three Jesuses actually, Ward 16
Schizophrenic patients of mine
Delusions that they're Christ
Leon, the youngest, walks in first
Looks the part   Skinny with long brown hair, beard
Except he chain smokes, Drum, hand rolled
Eyes bulge   Flicks his ciggie

> *You can call me Rex, R.I. Shit or Dung*
> *Dr. Righteous Idealed Shit*
> *At your service sir*

Put these men together
Absurdity of their claims
Essentially assist one another in healing
Sense of self challenged, controlled setting

> *My mother is my wife*
> *Madame Yeti   First Lady of the Universe*
> *Married 38 years*

How is that possible for a 36 year old man?—

> *Born married sir*

Only one Son of God
So anyone who believes himself to be Jesus

Suffers psychological affront
I'm saying the same things this crazy fool is saying
Therefore this must mean I am crazy too

*

Our daughter, 25
Doesn't think she's Jesus
But she was a Jew for Him
One Sovereign God
Existing in three persons
Father, Son, Holy Ghost
This was after Buddha and Krishna
Before her embrace of Single Life Force
The Great Mystery
Expressed in every human, animal, plant
Don't know which religion's
In rotation now

> *Honey, if you want to learn about the Bible*
> *I'll take you to Israel*
> *We'll learn together*

We believe she still lives
In Truchas, New Mexico   Changed her name:
Chenoa—dove   8000 feet above sea level
Dirt roads   Studio in a former church
Long wavy hair over a pottery wheel
Months we don't hear from her
Won't answer my letters or accept money
Calls collect

> *I'll only speak to Mom*

*

Then there's Joseph

Short, fat, bald Jesus   Coke bottle specs
Wife does not want him released
Declares Leon and Clyde in fact dead
Machines inside them
Produce these false claims
England will not be invaded

Rex and Clyde help me protect the stronghold

They are not against England

Just patients in a hospital, that's all

I am God and don't want
Anybody to worship me

In the recreation room
Among a hundred other patients
Sit together   Large table against wall
Free to wander aimlessly, watch TV.
Ping pong, play cards   Joseph always
In chair at the end   Leon
Chair next to Joseph, back to him
Rarely speak but trade tobacco
Clyde shares basket of fruit, his sister

Leon gazes at ten dollar bill
Enclosed in a letter, imaginary wife
I sent it to him

I have no use for money

Intensity of expression
          —What are you looking at?—
Two tiny droplets, corner of his eye
          —Is there something the matter with your eyes?—
                Oh, they're smarting sir
                So I'm enjoying some disinfectant
                The best in the world sir

One day our daughter just snapped,
Psychotic break
Grabbing strangers on the street
Charging oncoming traffic
Auditory, visual hallucinations, paranoia
Double locked, psychiatric ward
Effexor, Wellbutrin, Risperdal
Heavy eyed, out of focus
Smudged photograph of herself

What did you poison me with Dad

Came home for awhile
No job, not in school
Sneaking out to meet boyfriend
Love nest in the basement
Afraid to leave her alone

Then one day she's gone

Nothing for months, no contact
Then a package—
Addressed to me, clear plastic bag
All of her hair   A note:
Signed, Samson

*

Rather than come to the conclusion
None of them Jesus
Or one convincing others
They're not Jesus
Decided, Christ-like, divide
The awesome responsibility
Co-reign as Messiah

Christ of Salvation
Christ of Miracles
Christ of Service

Late at night, dorm
15 patients in bed
One of them snoring loudly

—Jesus Christ, quit the snoring!—

That wasn't me! It was him!

*

We hear nothing from her for a year
Letters to New Mexico returned
Addressee unknown
Then one day, a postcard
Foreign stamp, Israel
Addressed to me, her handwriting
No note

I smile

Church of the Mount, Jerusalem

THE THING IN THE BASEMENT

For Izzy

Company over for dinner
Freshwater prawns with snail butter
Our friend on his laptop   How simple
To invade thousands of systems   Ghostnet
I keep hearing banging in my basement   Gnarled
Light trying to burn my shoes   I'm the only one
That can see it   They're enjoying their aperitifs
I hear the mad beating of drums   Possessed breathing
Lightning under floorboards   The house shakes
My daughter still playing with her friend   Rolls
Her favorite blue ball   My wife wants me to pour refills
Wonders why I'm so fidgety   I stumble downstairs
The walls pulsate, living tissue   Something festers in mineral salts
Broods   Glaring red eyes lead me to a dark chamber I can see
A pulpy, tentacled head, wings, scaly arms, croaking voice
I'm below an onyx pedestal surrounded by red toads
Monoliths   I need to get home   I run past the vast Roman ruins
And then I see black spires in the distance   Supercomputer clusters
Blocks of gravity grids, terminals, vector processors, assemblages
Of chips and resistors   Beneath it all a shiny couch   A table
With amber glasses   Generators roar   I hold my ears   Careful
Not to slip on my daughter's ball

SNOW BALL

August 12, 1937
A four engine Soviet-made
Bolkhovitnov A-Bomber
Commodored by Sigismund Levanevsky
Five crew members
Disappears over shelf ice
Alaskan side of North Pole
Siberian radio picks up indistinct signals
Could be missing plane
Sigismund Levanevsky—Pilot, Adventurer
Hero of the Soviet Union
Known as the Russian Lindbergh

Soviet Government commissions the only man
Who can locate and rescue them
If they're still alive
Sir George Hubert Wilkins—Renowned Polar explorer,
Pilot, spy, geographer, newsreel cameraman, ornithologist
Holder of the Military Cross of the British Empire
Knighted by King George V
First person to fly across the Polar ice
From Point Barrow, Alaska to Spitsbergen, Norway

New York, prior to departure
Sir Hubert—bald, goatee, thin mustache
Consults Harold Morrow Sherman—
Novelist, lecturer, author of two Broadway plays
Student of mental powers
Long intrigued by phenomenon

Of mind to mind communication:
Telepathy
Unusual opportunity, put to test,
3400 miles apart
Thought transference appointments
Three nights a week
Sir Hubert's small plane, moonlit snowscapes,
Roof of the world
Send thoughts to the receiver:
Mr. Sherman—darkened study,
380 Riverside Drive, Manhattan
Furiously scribbles impressions—
Typewritten copies, dispatches carbon
Immediately to Sir Hubert

Sherman is electrified
A circuit has been closed
Between his mind and Sir Hubert's
A white mental motion picture screen
Hangs in the darkness of inner consciousness—
Flashed images
Sir Hubert's flying machine
Lockhead Electra 10E
Equipped with extra fuel tanks
Taxies down frozen river
In the clear moonlight
Rough ice throws heavy shadows

> *You turn some sort of instrument in your hand—Is it a*
> *   rangefinder?—*
> *Now had the phenomenon of white lights—like sparks—*
> *Seemed to appear in the dark*

After dinner at Keen's Chophouse
Friends ask Sherman
If it would inhibit his work
If they're seated in the study with him
The doctor, his wife Erica

And Sherman's wife
All sit on the sofa
Snowing outside
Sherman—thinning dark hair
Wearing double breasted suit
Brown cheviot
White linen handkerchief
Embroidered with HS monogram
Sits with his back to them
Facing the wall, scratches his nose
Doesn't notice
Shadows of snowflakes
Flicker across him

Tea with Lt. Governor
Joins Chief of the Northwest Mounted Police
Armistice Ball that evening
Formal affair
But Sir Hubert forgets to bring dress clothes
He accepts the loan
A man his size
His white tie and tails
Next morning, Mayor of Winnipeg
Presents Sir Hubert with
Badge of Honor
In a speech Sir Hubert points out
Spirit of comradeship and good fellowship
Has observed among all men
His dealings with so-called Bolsheviks of Russia—
Most gentlemanly
Snow flurries
Only one lady present
Wife of Captain Innes Taylor
Brushes snow off Sir Hubert
Pins the badge on his fleece coat
Front page of Winnipeg Tribune:
Charcoal likeness of Sir Hubert
Drawn days before by Miss Kathleen Shackleton

Sir Hubert leans against a pillow
Ivory double breasted dinner jacket, black tie
Gnarly hands folded on his lap

Social occasion—important people present—You appear
in evening wear yourself—Someone seems to pin some
thing on your coat lapel—You pleased with charcoal
likeness—See your face toward my left as I look at picture

A headache which persists
Causes Sherman concern
Possible interference receiving impressions
Thermal noise
Types quickly, his new musical comedy
To clear his mind

Something mechanical doesn't suit you—You glad it's
acting up now—
Rather than later—De-icing—Feeling strong here you
should watch this for protection

Sir Hubert—who has not received Sherman's dispatch yet—
Decides to fit and install on plane
Not a de-icer
But a nose cowling, keeps engine warm

Earlier in the evening
Sherman feels anxious
Dinner at the City Club
On his way home
Blaze in tenement
Six story building
A dozen Seagrave fire trucks
Pumper tankers
Volume of thick smoke
Long streams of flame

Licking at doorposts and windows
Flashes
Dark figures lean over a fire escape

Subway uptown
Wicker seats, porcelain covered strap poles
Sherman tries to keep his mind clear
Rubs his nose
Carefully reads the ads:
Wrigley's Gum: The Spearmint Girl
With the Wriggly Eyes
Burnett's Vanilla
But he suddenly sees a fire
Flaring against the black void of his inner mind

Point Barrow, Alaska
Sir Hubert lands his machine
In the darkness, ice lagoon
On the south side a cluster of Eskimo shacks and tents
Further off—the wireless station
Church and school yard

Locals bring him warm reindeer skins
About to turn in for the night
Startled by fire alarm
Sir Hubert peeks out the window
White house blazing in the night
Throws reflection over snow and ice
Chimney and roof collapse
Crowd gathers
Figures hurry toward flames
Their shadows lengthen
Bitter cold, stiff breeze blowing
Men shovel snow on the fire

Back in New York
Harold Sherman is in his pajamas

Pacing his study
Scribbles on back of envelope, a napkin
But now he's leaning down
Reaching for the floor of his study
Like he's bowing
Harold Sherman is about to toss snow

KNOWLEDGE

I'm nearby   Haven't been there in years
Gray, getting dark, some frozen rain
I call my wife   I will be home late
She and my daughter miss me
I wander around the campus   No one around
Getting darker, sooty snowflakes
I can hear the rattle of dead leaves
Buildings look the same: The East Tower, The Commons,
Bogart Hall   Violent wind and lightning   Chunks
Of black ice   I duck in to my old dorm   A young woman
Shakes me   Calls me by my name   She knows me, kisses me
Has soft skin, dark hair, ponytail, overalls   She's
Concerned about me   Wants to take me to the infirmary
I tell her I'm married, a father   She tugs at me   Why
Won't I listen   Sobs, slaps my face   Outside, the pink buds
Of cherry trees   But overgrown blue vines entangle the dorms
Ostriches charge across the Quad, students riding them
And it's raining falling ash   I stagger towards The Science Building
Meteors everywhere   Gargoyles swoop down, trying to snatch me
I hear laughter, ostrich grunts   I'm in a lab   No one here
I walk among the pendulums, electroscopes and pulleys
Past resistance boxes, industrial coils   I rifle through some textbooks
Diagrams of wavelengths, electron shells, light cones   The ceiling cracks

SILENCE

For my friend Seb Doubinsky

1. THE ENCOUNTER

December 26, 1980
Shortly after midnight
Large joint US and British Air Force base
Bentwaters
80 miles Northeast of London
81st Tactical Flight Wing
In charge of security
My radio—some lights seen
Rendlesham Forest
Just outside gate of base

Sergeant, whatever it was didn't crash
It landed

Order Airmen First Class
Cabansag and Burroughs
To respond with me
Bright light pulses
An object
Clearing on forest floor
Blue yellow red swirls
As we approach on foot
Silhouetted
Triangular craft

9 feet long
Six and a half feet high

Radio difficulties, static
I send Airman Cabansag further back
Relay messages—Central Security Control
Air around us electrically charged
Hair stands up, dances on our skin
No sound
Nothing in my training
Prepares me for what we're witnessing

No type of aircraft I've ever seen

After 10 minutes
No apparent aggression
Craft non-hostile
Following security protocol
Complete on-site investigation
Full physical examination of craft
Walk around it

My God what is this thing?

Small amount of white light
Peers out bottom
At left side center, bluish light
Other side, red
Take two rolls, black and white film
Notebooks entries, sketches
Relay messages to CSC
I'm trying to stay calm
Focused

I'm on top of the craft
Fabric of shell
Smooth, opaque like black glass
Symbols, etched or engraved

Texture of sandpaper
Diamond cut
Triangle in center
Two small solid, black circles

I touch them
They're warm

Something downloads in to my head
Or it feels that way
I might have blacked out
Feel like I'm underwater
Lights start to get brighter
Still no sound
I jump down, white lights
Take defensive positions
Lifts off ground
250 feet over tops of trees
Then—Gone
I write in my notebook
Speed: Impossible

Airman Burroughs:
How are we going to explain this man?
How?

II. CONTAINMENT

Airman Burroughs and I
Instructed to report
To Shift Commander's office
Assistant Operations Officer
Will debrief us
Speaks in very calm, steady voice

Can you gentlemen explain to me
What happened out there?

We describe the events
But leave out the symbols
I don't know why

Learn that others at the base
All trained observers
Witnessed the takeoff
The lights disappear
But didn't get close like us

When it took off I felt alone

After a long pause
Calm, taps his pencil on the desk

Gentlemen, what you say
You experienced tonight
Is no longer able to be reported
Through Air Force channels
Some things are best left unsaid

Instructs us to be quiet about it
No further discussion allowed

Forget it ever happened

III. FOG

I drop my film off
At the base lab
But never get them back
Told they didn't come out

Fogged
Overexposed

I take Burroughs home
He's agitated about the whole thing

Runs his fingers through his dark hair
Inhales his cigarette, slaps the dashboard

Why are they in denial man?
         —Because they don't know what it is
This is fucked up man

When I get home
I don't tell my wife
Keep seeing a whirlpool of digits in my head
Ones and zeros, various sizes
Choppy waves
An ocean during a storm

IV. RETURN TO THE SITE

The next morning
I return to the landing site
Ordered to look for physical evidence

Broken branches
Scorch marks on trees
Facing the site
Three indentations in the ground
Marks left by landing gear
Three corners of a triangle

Relieved to find proof
It really happened

Take more pictures
Leave, come back
Make plaster casts
Of the indentations
Which I keep for myself

Late afternoon
Drive in to village of Ipswich

Where I live
Buy groceries
Get my routine back

Old farmer stables
Reflect in glass panels
Of the Willis Building
Stroll by the Marina
Strung lights, bobbing
Fairline boats, spirit yachts
An old man
Torn coat, eye patch
Homeless and Hungry, God Bless
His hand outstretched
Startles me
When he grabs my shoulder
And smiles

I go home that night
Feel like I'm thousands of fathoms
Underwater
Trying to swim up
So I can breathe
Scribble 12 pages of digits
Mostly zeros and ones

Is it some sort of binary code?
Telepathic download

Or am I just crazy?

I'm not going to tell them

v. It Comes Back

That same night at the base
I'm not there
Burroughs is

61

Everyone sees it
Over 80 Airmen

A red oval light
Looks like an eye
Lt. Colonel Halt and his men
Pursue through the woods
Until it crosses a farmer's field
Explodes in to five white objects

Nothing shows up on radar

Then another glowing orb
Emits a thin beam
Touches the ground near their feet

Disappears

VI. DEBRIEF AGAIN

I'm directed to report
To the Office of Special Investigations
0900 in the morning
Meet with a couple of agents
An hour and a half
Tell them the story
From two nights before

Seem content with the information
I provide them
No problem with the fact
That I had seen a craft

I don't tell them
About the symbols
That I touched them
Or about the digits

Over the next few days
Everyone nervous
Damage control

Do not talk
Or your career will be ruined

First week in January
Told to ignore any kind of activity
Perimeter of gate
Near the landing site

Special team going to do
Some overdue electronics work
Cordoned off, wooden wall

They're not wearing uniforms
They're wearing civilian clothes

VII. LEAK

A few years later
Memorandum to British Ministry of Defense
From Lt. Colonel Holt is released
Freedom of Information Act
Events of late December, 1980
Are made public
My name is included
I am being tied to it

Always stayed quiet
All of us have
27 military honors
Letter of Appreciation from the President

They thought damage control was complete
Contained the situation

Now I read other accounts
Quoting people who claim
To be primary witnesses
And they weren't
Saying certain events happened
That didn't
CNN, Unsolved Mysteries, books, magazines

The Air Force stays silent
Like the mysterious craft
On that cold December night

I'm reassigned to Grissom Air Force Base, Indiana
My family and I
Housing on the base
And there I find, quite by accident,
Embedded in the living room wall
A listening device, a bug
Smaller than a quarter
Green metallic on one side
Chrome on the other

My mail is tampered with
Things opened, resealed

Downtown Kokomo
Meeting a friend I trust
To show him the bug
Markland and Main Area
Believe it or not
This little thing has a range of 3000 feet
When I leave—a young, homeless woman
African American
Never seen her before
Shopping cart, shivering inside
A black garbage bag
Holds out her hand
Shaking, abnormally large eyes

For some reason
I give her a ten

VIII. HYPNOSIS

The mid 1990's
I retire from the Air Force
Hypnotized by my teenage daughter's psychiatrist
Feel like more happened to me
That I can't recall

The debriefing, December, 1980
Two OSI agents
But then those two leave
And two other officials
One American, one British
Ask me, again, recount the story

Would I mind being given
A shot of something
Then tell my story again
While they tape record it

If that's what it takes
But I don't like shots

It's standard procedure
Not to worry about it
We've done it before

Lie down on a walnut table
British guy gets the needle ready
Lift arm
Shot of sodium pentothal

Ask repeatedly
Trajectory of the craft
Its speed and approach

Calmly repeat over and over
Did not see any of that
Craft was already on the ground

Answer questions
About the symbols
Ask if they are engraved on surface
Yes
Did I write down any digits, any binary code

They know what I've seen
Knew it already

What do you understand about the code?

> *I'm the interpreter. They need interpreters. The lights.*

You are an interpreter?

> *Yes.   They are time travelers.   They are us.*

They are us from . . .

> *The future.*

What do they need?

> *Not sure.   Has to do with chromosomes.   They take it. Other people's bodies.*

Did they take it from you?

> *Didn't.   They are having problems. By touching these things I activated something.*
>
> *It was repairing itself*
> *All they wanted was a place to stay awhile*
> *It repaired itself*

They need speed to travel

To travel through time?

To go backwards. They can't go forward.
It's impossible to go into the future.

These ships can go back forty to fifty thousand
years
Can't go much further. Might not be able to get
back.

Chromosomes gathered for different reasons
Been coming for a long time
30 to 40,000 years
Trying to sustain their children in the future
Hairless, humanoid bodies, pale skin
Claw-like hands, 4 fingers
Large eyes
To take in more light
Because the future will be different

IX. HI BRASIL

After 30 years
I decide to entrust
12 pages of digits
To two different computer programmers

Is this a random series of numbers
Or some sort of numerical message,
Code?

52 09 42.32 N
13 13 12.69 W
Longitude, latitude
Mythical phantom island

West of Ireland
The other Atlantis
Hi Brasil

Catalan map of 1481
Illa de brasil
Last supposed sighting—1872
Superior technology
Vibrational healing
Those who visited
Returned with tales of
Gold roofed towers, domes
Appears and then vanishes
Perfect circle
With a semi circular channel
Through the center

I'm on a research vessel
Glistening blue waters
Advanced digital communication
Search for sunken city

Satellite-integrated ocean bottom
Positing systems
High precision side scan
Double frequency sonar

High resolution images
Symmetrical architecture
Roads, buildings

When a fog comes up

We watch on the monitor
Something configure—
A triangle, a pyramid
Silent

VR

For my friend Tad Williams

Fierce flashes of lightning
But no rain   The desert cold and dark
Hiding in marble caves so the Fengkas don't
Root us out   Bat-like but laser eyes   They shriek
Glide over the mountains   Riding wind and electricity
Here we're warriors   Travelled many lands
Evergreens thousands of feet tall, crystal waterfalls
A red sky with five moons   I'm 6'5, black haired,
Sullen-eyed, bronze skin   An outlaw, a slayer
Here I have buddies   My best friend   Simone Alexander
Shapeshifter   Her green eyes glow at night   In the light
Of the moon   A long thin scar, the side of her face
Demon Hunter Kinu, the mutant vampire Eclipse
Steel Maiden—Invulnerable to harm   Eric Vrai Skorch
Bounty hunter, gunman   Not sure who some of them
Really are   Simone, a bank clerk Johannesburg   Single mom
Always pops offline   For days sometimes   Picks up her two girls
Damned Fiat keeps breaking down   Kinu, Perth, Australia
His butt   Kicked At school   Eric, car dealer, upstate New York
Too many French fries   Frigid winters   Then there's Skee
Bored, waiting for the next ambush   Campfire smoke
I stare at him   A shroud, he has no mouth   Can only hear him
breathing   Bubbles from the deep sea   Don't know if he is a
Visitor like us or something from here   A Puppet   In the real
world we all wear the headsets   I am here all of the time
My body broken   They don't know I'm 15   A fatal blood
disorder   Bed ridden   I lie about my age   My own software

company   A millionaire   My parents hope in death my mind will
somehow stay here   Forever   With my mates   Fending off
gladiators in pearl coliseums   Trees of silk   Platinum glaciers
Guiding giant albatrosses over pink oceans   Coral Islands
Mushroom towers in Plasma clouds   To the fringes   The outer
continents   Where worlds beget worlds   Stellar remnants
Dark matter   Spiral galaxies

GENUINE FAKE

For Lenora

The morning they came to arrest me
Pouring rain   I asked the detective
Can I walk my son to the school bus
I forget my raincoat   When I return
They've ransacked the farmhouse
Deny Everything But one of them hands me
Unposted letter, my briefcase
To my accomplice, the Professor
I want out of this ugly business
Dated three years ago

Paintings all over the floor
The Detective Sergeant, the one
Politely interrogating me, has three kids
Treasurer of Acorn Painting Club
These are exquisite
Do you like this one? Charcoal of my daughter
He nods, points to the others, knock offs by me:
Vibrant primary colored Chagalls
Simple primitive Dubbufet, Picassos
I confess on the spot
200 forgeries, style of nine modern masters
Sold through auction houses: Sothebys,
Christies, reputable dealers: London, Paris, New York
We fooled them all

My wife abandoned me, our little boy and girl
I'm broke   Teach art in local school
All day, other people's children
No time for my own
Need a way to work from home
No one interested in my paintings
Landscapes: Staffordshire countryside,
Portraits of neighbors   Friend offers $400
Copy a canvas by Post Impressionist Raoul Dufy
Yachting scene, sparkling view of French Riviera
Heightened ambient light   Driving to school
He calls   *It's tricking experts!*
Place classified ad: *Genuine Fakes*
19th and 20th Century, only $240

Enter the Professor
Answers my ad
Bought new house
Decorate, style of Matisse and Paul Klee
Could I copy French cubist Albert Gleizes
Calls me   Christies, worth $38,000
I can't believe it   Are you aware
It's painted in Dulux, household emulsion?
Meet for coffee   Drizzling
Pencil moustache, mohair coat
Expensive handmade shoes
Drives a Bristol motor car
Claims he's an agent, Israeli Secret Service
Physicist, Consultant for Defense Department
Invents gadgets—chemical warfare suit
Folds into size of golf ball

He'll sell my paintings
Pass them off as real thing
Only dead artists
Offers me half
Could make more selling one fake
Than whole year, supply teaching

I'm cash strapped
No one's getting hurt
What would you do?

I take the money

Neighbors might see me at my easel
Constant fear of exposure
Paint at night, in the cellar
My own addiction terrifies me
Meet the Professor, Euston Station
Raining   I need a new raincoat
Deliver rolled canvas, Picasso I made up
New piece every six weeks
Have a pint together   Turmoil of my divorce
Raising children alone Advice, comforts me
Solo trips to Coventry Cathedral
Copy Graham Sutherland's studies
Huge tapestry—Christ in His Glory
Surround myself with books
Know everything, where artist was
What he was doing   Did he have a wife
Perfectionists' desire, near perfect art
Drive to Liverpool   Meditate
Giacometti exhibition, Swiss surrealist
Five hours   Quick streaks—
Downpour of himself/myself
Same cotton duck canvas he used
Now I water down emulsion
KY lubricant jelly, authentic looking glaze
Sells for 175K

We're in the board room of the Tate
The Professor and I, his guest
Arrive, chauffer driven Bentley
Private viewing for trustees
Two white gloved curators
Carry museum's latest acquisition

Paintings of sea gulls
Highly regarded, little known fifties French artist
Roger Bisierre donated by distinguished scientist,
Businessman—The Professor
Painted by yours truly two weeks earlier
Ordinary emulsion, turpentine, linseed oil
Framed with leftover wood, construction on my barn
Smearing of dust from vacuum cleaner bag

Donations give the Professor access
Reading room of the Tate,
Victoria and Albert Museum
Insert photographs of my paintings—
Files and card indexes
Give pictures instant heritage
From creation, purchases, exhibitions
To current ownership
Altering provenance of genuine paintings

Why should the price
Of a luminous work of art crash
Just because it's by a nobody like me?

When the police raid the Professor's house,
Reigate, London suburb, kitchen table
Two catalogues missing from the V and A Art Library
Rubber stamps, authenticity seals—
Tate and Order of Monastic Priests
Receipts for sales of paintings
Across continents, going back decades
And the more mundane instruments of forgery:
Scissors, razors, glue, tape, correction fluid

I'm sentenced to one year
Draw pictures—fellow inmates, the warden
Exchange for phone cards
Bleak pencil drawing

A View Over Brixton Prison
Released, good behavior   A new wife
Three more kids   Energetic german shepherd
Named Henry   Rambling farmhouse
Fakes hang everywhere   My wife
Clad in Edwardian dress   Family
On an evening walk, style of Miro

I'm at my opening
Air Gallery, London's Mayfair
Genuine Fakes   Hung with Modiglianis,
Several Picassos   New to my repertoire:
Monet, Renoir, Cezanne   Sell for 50K a piece
Crowded, lots of media—rainy night
No other forger worked so prodigiously,
So many styles   At the book signing
A young man, internet print out
Online gallery, Giacometti abstract
Attributed to me   Swirling whites and gray
Entitled *Apples on a Stool, 1949*
Looks unfinished   I tell him it's not by me
A knock off   *What are you going to do?*
Wish the artist luck

In the gift shop
My Monet water lilies
Coffee mugs, cards, calendars
Blurry, edgeless forms
Shimmering with reflection
Clouds overhead
Panoply of blues, greens
Lavenders, creams and pinks
They also sell ties, handkerchiefs
And then I see the raincoats
With my water lilies too
And I buy one

TRANSPARENCY

Nighttime   Dreamland   The Ranch   Thousands of files
Loaded on trucks   A new 15,000 foot runway   18 new hangars
New tank systems   Cryogenic liquid methane   Antigravity
reactors   White balls of light seen from town, spherical,
transparent   If I can just get them to admit it, to formally
acknowledge   Like the barbell-shaped   Object over a highway,
Wakeeny, Kansas Heibe Sheng, China   A delta shaped craft with
lights   The 1986 San Paulo sighting   Some 250 eyewitnesses
The Trumbull Ohio Disturbance   Low flying multi-colored ones
My sister calls   Dad's back in the hospital   I tell her sacrifices
have to be made   The truth is more important   This is history's
major event and I'm sleeping on a friend's floor, end of story
1974, Coyanne, Mexico Mexico's Roswell   A mid-air collision
An object and small plane   A flatbed truck   Looked like two
saucers joined together   Radar tracked it, 2500 miles an hour
Bunch of dead Mexican Soldiers   Biohazard suits   The truck
with the craft dangling from an unmarked CH-53 Sea Stallion
helicopter   One of ours   We took it in to the heartland   This
year's X-Conference   I have three weeks   All nighters   Chinese
take out   We have an astronaut   An ultimatum to the President
Transparency   Turn over the files   They won't take my credit
card   I owe ten grand   The Phoenix Lights   Stephenville
Several dozen people   A pilot   All over radar   Large, silent
object, flying low   Fighter jets   Chasing it   I'm collecting a
million faxes by May   My sister, more messages   A phone
interview   I've never seen one myself This is an embargo on
the truth   We have the right to know   Where do you think all
of this technology comes from   With all due respect Collins is
just an historian   I'm an activist, a lobbyist   I do the heavy

Lifting   Of course there have been abductions   Large bald heads,
small sunken eyes, thin lipless mouths, devoid of teeth, earholes
Gray skinned   Large black wrap around eyes   Vertical pupils
Mouth is a slit, continually opens and closes, fish gills   Seated
on one legged stools   White almost translucent skin, blond eye
lashes   3 meters wide   Transparent spherical craft   Skin pinkish,
rest looks purple and bruised   Gourdos   The feared gray
species   Human-alien hybrids   Phantom pregnancies   Systematic
Interbreeding   I'm in Bethesda, exhausted   Trying to sleep   A
supporter's pull out couch   Noises and lights   Must be garbage
trucks or police cruisers   I look through the blinds   A craft
flat, octagon shaped   Must be 400 feet long   Two large lights
Bright like landing lights but solid blue   And five UH-60 Black
Hawk helicopters   Soldiers repelling   The top and bottom tower
lights of the mother ship   Strobing   I cannot see my hands

THE VEIL

She wears a patch over one eye
Doesn't see the knife in the air
But the sound of it
The *thunk*
Still gets to her during performance
Develops a twitch

My stage name is The Throw Master
Wear a black tuxedo
White turban on my head
Circuses, sideshows, cabaret, burlesque
World's fastest
Most accurate knife thrower

Hurl blades around Target Girl
Strapped to spinning wheel
The Wheel of Death

Painproof Rubber Girl
Scantily clad in blood red
(Obvious reasons)
Aim for the balloon between her legs
Graze one limb
Draw a bit of blood
Increasing bouts of flinching
Less of her flesh can be exposed

I can't do this anymore
Find a new Target Girl

Fling knives, machetes, tomahawks
Holder of 16 world records
Including most blades thrown
Around human target, one minute

Stiltwalker
Own a billiard hall
An ordained minister
Run a wedding business
Marry couples
Then entertain the guests—
My impalement art

New Target Girl answers my ad
The Hula Harlot
Professional Hula Hooper
Holder of 2 world records herself
The Flamingo, Fire Hooping
Pale skin, purple lipstick

I'm not scared of knife throws at all
And I'm the girl who won't go on a roller coaster

Spread eagled to wheel
Wide leather straps
Head secured in a vise
Like the electric chair

Give it a vigorous spin
Clutch blades in my left hand
Step back seven feet
The Throw Master's flawless rhythm
So cleanly—
Slices through ash of cigarette
Dangling out of her mouth

Now I will be
First impalement artist, 32 years—

Most dangerous act of all
Televised live—
Spinning wheel of death with Target Girl
Hidden behind paper veil

I've looked at this as an enigma
Huge mystery
How can someone throw knives
Through a veil
Without seeing the girl
Visual or audio clues

Has to be something

Months of re-engineering my wheel
Advice from physicist, an engineer
Expert in theater equipment

Practice with fiberglass mannequin
White figure strapped to large wooden wheel
My backyard
Cover entire contraption
Sheet of opaque butcher block paper

The Hula Harlot:
He's not some crazed man throwing knives

The Throw Master
Live before studio audience
Fencer's mask to protect her
Secured to veiled wheel

Given a terrific push—
Raise recurved Persian fighting blade
Just before the forearm
Is horizontal to ground
Precise moment it's perpendicular—

Slips from hand

One woman in audience
Screams **NO!**
Another shouts **OH MY GOD!**

I see her, unmistakably,
Behind giant canopy
Fitted bra
Fringe of beads and sequins
Shimming vibration of hips
Lifts her arms

Shadows of Isis wings

Hunter

Dusk   In the dead river
Standing on an old wooden door
I float to shore   The moon, behind clouds,
Glosses the sediment   I have my pistol,
Silver bullets, ivory crucifix, crossbow   The city
All darkness   But I see you, even from here
A shadow a top a crumbled building   The red flares
Of your eyes   Salisbury, ages ago, before all of this
Worshipping with my wife, two girls   The Morning Prayer,
Psalm 95   Strength of salvation   The girls singing
White muslin, lace, periwinkle blue   I float closer
Large, membraned wings, demon eyes   You see me
Snarls, groans   One night beneath the spires and transept
Of the cathedral   We buried you alive   Still a man,
Pounding in terror, the bubbling of gases, finger marks
In the coffin   Now I see only mist where you crouch
Molecules so diffuse you can pass through walls   And from
Clouds of dust Spectral wolves, ghost bats, gangrels
Because of you my youngest daughter, a child years later
My dagger in her heart   Bloodshot eyes, gnash teeth
Behind me, lying in the river, the twisted steel of
A suspension bridge   I rise   Walk on vapor   Clutching
The last vial of holy water   The moon shines   A chunk of it
Blown off   You, your legions, descend from rubble
Shrieks Growls   A wall of flame
I load the wooden bolt in to the crossbow

ZOMBIE

Night   I'm wandering along the side
Of a highway, searching for vagrants,
Trailer parks, easy human flesh   During
Lunch hour at a morgue I snuck
Brains, hearts, livers   Scraps from the dumpster
Maggots, discolored eyes, open wounds   Outside
The Cozy Inn Lounge   The light of neon martinis
I peek in the window   A couple slow dances
My wife the night we first met   Tight black jeans,
An army green crop shirt, high heels   A couple
Staggers outside   She, blonde, barely able to stand,
Holding the man   I don't let them see my lacerations,
Blistered skin   Now I'm hungry   In the ironweed, bull thistle
Beer bottles   My slow, shambling gait   Gutteral moan
That night we played pool, danced to Endless Love
Her platinum skin   Ready to gorge

EYEBALL

While waiting for my daughter
And two grandsons to visit
I read they've declassified
Our secret film unit
1352nd Photography Squadron
Thousands of blinding flashes
Fireballs   Fiery images
Nuclear test explosions
200 Atmospheric blasts—
Atomic Cameramen

Aren't many of us left
Most dead from cancer

Visits me once a week
Make sure I'm still functioning
After Mother died
Brings soup or favorite turkey sandwich
Boys playing on the carpet
Chew lemon Starburst, candy eyeballs
Godzilla action figure
Topples my bowling trophies
Crumbling buildings
Flee in terror
Divorced, always fidgets with purse
Cherry bomb lip gloss

Blames Mother and me
Never accepted him
Japanese man   Both struggling actors
Implode

II.

6500 secret films
Between 1946-1962
Inconspicuous building
Surrounded by lush greenery
Laurel Canyon
Neighbors suspicious
Lights on all the time

For scientists investigating
Nature of nuclear explosion
Federal and Congressional leaders
Control appropriation of atomic funds—
Special viewings

Sound stages, 3 screening rooms
Optical printing capabilities
17 climate controlled film vaults
3D, Cinemascope, Stereophonic Sound
Personal bomb shelter, helicopter pad
Dispatched to remote South Pacific atolls
Dusty Nevada ridge tops
Fastex cameras running up to
10,000 frames per second
Analyze blast forces
Measure movement as a function of time
Waiting for aftershock

III.

My daughter's husband
A bit part

Japanese TV dorama
Handsome male protagonist
Heals sick woman
With his love
In real life
His love radiates beyond the show—
Bombshell co-star, their next door neighbor

Max, the older boy, licking a whirlpop
Watches movie, his iPod
I need my glasses
Walking With Dinosaurs
T-Rex in fierce battle
Serious bite punctures
Bone of its snout

> *Grandpa, you know how they died, the dinosaurs?*
> *No, you tell me Max*

Chixulub asteroid
Strikes the earth
100 million megatons of force
Volcanic eruptions
Massive earthquakes, tsunamis
Scalding acid downpours
White hot debris falling all over the world

IV.

We were the Atomic Cameramen

Five of us stand at ground zero
I wear a baseball cap
Thickest welders goggles
A still camera, two motion picture 35mm Eyemos
10,000 feet above us
First comes the light

86

Brightest I have ever seen
Every object loses color

Another time
I'm flying directly over explosion
Aim the camera
My goggles fall apart before the blast
Fireball, searing hot flash
Desert floor turns to glass
Hold hand over my eyes
I can see bone through my skin

Redwing Cherokee, 1956
3.8 megatons
K-24 camera with 20 inch lens
Dominic Sunset, 1962, Christmas Island
Rapatronic camera—initial burst of energy
First one millionth of a second

Crescent shaped shockwaves

We blow up mock towns
2 story brick houses
Thermal effects on lumber and plywood
Glass shatters
Rayon drapery burned
Wool rug fused and charred
Electrical towers, telephone polls snap
Yellow school bus: First, it catches fire
Then wind blows it out
Flare up

Allowed to witness
Not photograph
First H-Bomb detonation

One thousand times more powerful
Than atomic blasts

Twenty miles away
Eerie glow in the sky, swirling—
Color of candy corn

V.

We're all ducking
From a T-Rex
Peering in to my window
Drive us out of my condo
For an ambush
7 tons, 18 feet high

Most powerful jaw ever Grandpa
To be continued next week Boys

After they leave I sit down
Sip cold tea
The first eyewitness accounts
About Nagasaki—
Children falling in all directions
Like bowling pins
Slap their burning school uniforms
Powerful winds
Try to walk, stumble over a tree
Point to large form on the ground
Look over there
It's escaped from the zoo
An alligator!
Hold a rock above their heads
Approach it
Face looking up is human
Pleads for water
No clothing or hair
Scale-like burns cover its head and body
Skin around its eyes burned away
Leaving only eyeballs

LEOPARD MEN

Coast of Maine   The family lodge
On one side the lighthouse, harbor seals, terns
On the other—a lake full of moon   Dinner
My big brother and I would watch our great aunt Beatrice,
Perfect gray bun, always fondle her pendant, the Bavarian order
Of St. George   A knight stabbing a dragon   We'd sneak off
To the Rec House   Walnut panels, Brunswick billiard table,
The mounted heads of white tail deer, moose, my great grandfather's
Prize cape water buffalo   And hide behind a sliding door   One night
We heard high pitched cackling laughs, whopping sounds
Coming from the Rec House   In splintering light we saw hyenas
Darting back and forth, gangling   Beckoning us inside, behind
Our secret sliding door   We crawled past black limestone cats,
Lion goddesses, alabaster vessels, sphinxes   Now we're on
The River Congo   Our great grandfather Sir John's famed steel barge,
His quest for the legendary Leopard Men, cannibals   Straw mats
With sacks of sugar and salt, malaria pills, cookie tins   Villagers
Paddling up in dug out canoes   A five foot long crocodile, jaws roped shut
Blackened monkey carcasses, their eyes and mouths wide open as if
Smoked alive   We thread our way through a dark labyrinth of aisles
Drumbeats announcing our arrival   Trees with majestic canopies, air heavy,
The river a sheet of glass spreading all around us   Tree silhouettes,
Fat, sluggish moths, dragonflies, mosquito swarms   Color reduced to
Black and gray and then dusk   The river lilac, bleeding red, running
Into purple   Sir John regales us with chocolate, encounters
With the Leopard Men, slaying a sea serpent   Grasping the pendant
He will one day bequeath to our great aunt   Now we're back in Maine
The long dinner table   Our great aunt twirls the pendant
She too went on expeditions   But my brother and I can't sleep

89

We're crawling again   Uncle Burt and we're on balsa wood rafts
In search of the source of the Amazon   Rapids, snakes, headhunters
My uncle singing the Eton Boating Song   Roast monkey, bamboo
shoots and snails   He carries a backpack and a briefcase
Only drinks water from puddles   Years later, with my wife and kids
Detroit
We're snowed in   My daughter clutches her chameleon tank   Storms
and floods
On the east coast   Whole houses on the eastern seaboard swallowed by
the sea
My brother calls   But I send it to voicemail   It's been too many years
I imagine our lodge sliding in   The billiard table, moose heads, hyenas
Our secret doorway Everything taking on water Our great aunt Beatrice
Eyes and mouth wide open   Losing the pendant

SHADOWS OVER CHINATOWN

My big brother Jeff and I
Race our stingrays, new Bruce Lee movie
The Way Of The Dragon
Dad refuses to drive us
My Schwinn Banana Bomber
Custom handlebars   His five speed Fastback
Popping wheelies, cutting through backyards
3 miles to Granada Theatre
Old art deco castle, peeling walls
Musky odor   Jeff, c's and d's in school,
No friends except me, loves movies —
Chinese movies   Constantly reads about them
Tells me once this theatre had doorman,
Frock coat, white gloves, waiting to open
Your car door, direct you to ticket booth
Passed from usher to usher   Flashlights,
Ornate lobby corridors, Egyptian palace

Before movie starts—Jeff has list
All things Bruce Lee can do, we can't:
Snatch a dime, person's open palm
Before they can close it, replace with penny
Break wooden board 6 inches thick
Striking speed from 3 feet,
Hands down by side, five hundredth of a second
"Be formless and shapeless like water
Now you put water in cup, it becomes the cup"

Or, as our favorite Honolulu detective
Charlie Chan put it:

Falling hurts least those who fly low

In the movie—Bruce, Hong Kong expat in Italy,
Kicks all kinds of ass
Local thugs muscle in, Chinese restaurant
Final fight scene:
Chuck Norris—imported martial arts assassin
Spectacular setting, Roman Coliseum
Meticulously choreographed
Flurry of kicks and punches

Some heads like hard nuts   Much better if well cracked

On the way home
Dive off our bikes
Snap kick like Bruce Lee
Jeff on the sidewalk, porky with freckles,
Blue windbreaker
Giggles, out of breath
Always sweats even if it's freezing

Every Sunday this fall
Dad makes him sit in front of TV
Two of them, football,
Even though it's Chinese Torture
Dad had law practice
Now owns couple of women's clothing stores
Lets me wear his tool belt
Gives us sips, can of Reingold
Stories about the War
Commanded mobile anti aircraft battery
Hop scotched across South Pacific,
Australia, Philippines, New Guinea
"It was an eye opener for me
I wouldn't ever take it back"

Jeff doesn't care
Rather be in our bedroom
Posters, still, lobby cards
Five Fingers of Death
Five Shaolin Masters
Ming the Merciless
And the fluid grace, sensuality
Of Anna May Wong
Played either naïve, self sacrificing butterfly
Or sly, deceitful dragon ladies
Here she is, in lounging robe, silk satin
Groundbreaking ceremony
Grauman's Chinese Theatre
Lotus shaped fountains, 30 foot dragon
Temple bells, jade heaven dogs
Anna fled Hollywood
Turned down by MGM, Chinese lead
Pearl S Buck's **The Good Earth**
Part given to Hungarian actress

Action speak louder than French

When he grows up
Jeff wants to go to Hollywood
Write and direct movies

Bring back Charlie Chan

My favorite photos
Besides the ones of Charlie Chan
The Evil Criminal Genius himself:
Dr. Fu Manchu
Tall, lean, feline
Stops at nothing to conquer the West
Weapons of choice: daggers, pythons,
Hammadryads, fungi and black spiders

No poison more deadly than ink

Our favorite actor to play
The Yellow Peril incarnate
Swedish actor Warner Oland
Better known for playing Al Jolson's
Orthodox Jewish Cantor father, first talkie
The Jazz Singer
And for his future role—Charlie Chan

Dad wants Jeff to go to football camp
Next summer — Full contact drills, scrimmages
Teaches teamwork, self discipline
Potential on the field and in life

Is Dad fucked in the head? I ain't going

Saturday nights
Jeff's old enough to babysit for me
Our ritual: Channel 9, 8 pm
Charlie Chan movies
I wear my Batman pajamas
Jeff wears panama hat like Charlie
Years later, both in college,
I send Jeff a real one, an Optimo—
Colonial panama hat   Exact kind
He wore: **Charlie Chan in Panama**

Chubby, inscrutable face, dark goatee
Middle aged Chinese American detective
Friendly and self effacing
Investigates and arrests villains, mostly whites
No fan of tea, prefers to drink sarsaparilla
Fortune cookie aphorisms

Truth like football
Receives many kicks before reaching goal

His Chinatown beat: booths and stalls

Along narrow winding streets
Opium dens, gambling parlors
Golden Gate Fortune Cookie Factory
Herbal shops, merchants and lanterns

Tonight's movie **Charlie Chan's Secret**
A missing heir, his family set to inherit millions
Séance and a ghostly glow, secret passage
Before body falls to floor
Abnormally large close ups of Charlie
Takes in possibly suspicious actions,
Those around him

Finding web of spider does not prove
Which spider spin web

The séance music just a radio receiver
Not manifestation from world beyond
Analysis of handkerchief: presence of
Genuine sulfate which glows
When exposed to light, ultra violet projector
Hidden behind mirror, mantelpiece across the room
Charlie catches sight (in mirror) of gun
Pointed in their direction
Pushes himself and Mrs. Lowell out of harm's way

Role of dead man requires very little acting

Now I'm visiting my brother
Divorced, his ex and two girls
Back in New Jersey
Just woken up, hung over,
Pull out couch, living room
Jeff's high rise, Hong Kong
His bedroom door's still closed
Pour myself a glass of water
Walls bare   A ladies red dragon silk robe
On the floor Boxes of DVDs everywhere

Chinese lettering, squiggly creatures:
G Force, Beverly Hills Chihuahua
Director of Marketing, Disney, all of China
I step out on the balcony
20th floor
Unobstructed view
Hong Kong Island skyline
Across Victoria Harbor
Down below—Olympic sized pool, tennis courts,
Luxury mall   And beyond—clutter of narrow streets,
Shopping districts, a pet store, Karaoke lounges
I'm holding Charlie's panama hat
One I gave Jeff in college
Found it on kitchen counter
Crease, center of crown from being rolled up
I put it on

TELL THEM WHAT I SAW

They are trying to revive me
Floating above the Resus Area I am part
Of a study—The Division of Perceptual Research
The white patches of heaven on my chest
Emergency medical physicians, nurses, technicians
Lean over me   Outside I can see my wife, two grown sons
Weeping, a prayer circle   Psalm 34:19 The Lord
Always brings us through   My son's track and field gear
I'm above the nurses station   Laughter, tonight's double date
At the Well   My mind more clear   Bright light everywhere
The doctor motions for the defibrillator paddles to shock me back
I remember, the boys little, we climbed Mt. Greylock—miles
Of farms, the curve of the earth   They commence cardiopulmonary
Resuscitation, even pound my chest I can see the video monitors
Placed at the top of the ceiling   Psi Effects Altered States
Of consciousness   If I come back, tell them what I saw 15 feet
Above: Two cheetahs
Racing across a great yellow plain   A finish line   Kingdom of Light

Conference Room

A rainforest surrounds us   Toucans, mist, spider monkeys leap in
trees   We can not see each other   Collaborate as if in the same
room   But we're avatars   Digital three dimensional head busts
Immersive virtual environment   A webinar   Launch of a new
secret chip   Directive from HQ—secure the accounts   Sony,
Toshiba, Trolltech   We can look in each other's eyes
Team's never met for real   A two toed sloth hanging upside
down behind her, Lucy preps us.—nervous giggles   Red hair, left
cheek—tattoo of a gargoyle   Wonder if it's real, if she's single
Poured in to silicon wafers, baked   I will be chief negotiator,
Trolltech   Lunch break   Feeling tense, drive my Tundra
down   Toolson's General and Feed   An egg salad sandwich,
bread, coffee   Get stares   A woman says: Rte 3, a rabid
coyote dragged a dachshund carcass   Back in the conference
room my avatar five inches taller for Trolltech   Three of them
arrive   Trolls—gray, shaggy   Power point presentation
Until now semiconductors leaked current   The licensing fee
Rude snickers   I reiterate the price, our loyal partners   No, they
won't agree   Guffaws, tails beating   Insulting   One of them
scampers under the table   I try to snatch him   Chortles   My
face reddens   Head swells   I grab him by the throat   He's
snarling   I recoil, flash teeth   Then bite

DARK MISSION

Today we'll discover water   A kinetic explosion—upper stage
Of LRO launch vehicle, the Centaur,   Ramming the moon, 2
miles per second   A plume of lunar dust, shattered rock
Ice, eons of cometary impacts   Hidden until now
Millions watching—CNN, classrooms, wife, two boys, President
himself   But we've piggybacked another mission, the real one,
classified   This past Christmas   An empty beach, my boys
Waves whipping the rocks   Sand fortresses, canals, Star Wars
assault vehicles   My older son: Are there aliens on the Moon?
Rises behind fog, mist like a rubbing   No, of course not
Can't tell him I've seen the images—,   Apollo, Lunar Orbiters,
Clementine Satellite   Not the blur/smudge tampering for the public
Tiered, rectilinear structures   Western edge, Sea of Tranquility—
grid-like patterns, girders of collapsed buildings, casting shadows
A second satellite, LCROSS, tears away from the first   Towards
the fierce darkness   Moon's south pole   Bridges
spanning chasms, two narrow filaments, glass fragments, ruins of
ancient domes   The Shard   World witnesses the
Centaur crash in to the surface   Upward jetting dust, ice vapors—
        hovering   An inverted cone of light, 10 miles high
But on the far side, a bunker bomb   Breaking walls, debris,
punching a hole in the roof   Dome shattered   When I get
home that night I tell them what a miracle it was, the cascade of
water   How when there's barely an atmosphere everything is
so clear

PAST LIFE

The nightmares haven't stopped
Kicking, thrashing His mother wakes
Him, he's screaming 3 year old boy, otherwise
Happy toddler Flopping around in his bed
Like a broken power line Then the actual words:
"Plane on fire! Blue Bear! Little man can't get out!"
At Hobby Lobby—lifts a balsa wood propeller plane out of
The bin "That's not a bomb Mommy. That's a drop tank"
Distinguish World War II planes—P-51 Mustangs, Spitfires, Wildcats
Drowsy in bed, reveals that he flew a Corsair, Japanese shot him down,
Blue bear again, the name of the ship he took off from   With my wrinkled
Hands I dust off the photo frame, bleached shot of him, smiling from
The cockpit—65 years ago

These young parents of a boy, hearing the memories of my decades
Lost older brother Boy's father, an oil executive, doesn't know
Why he is at this reunion   This is crazy   USS Natoma Bay
San Diego, Grant Hill ballroom   Frail veterans at tables:
Maps, journals, photographs   Chasing his son's memories, not yet
Potty trained   My brother's memories   No one knows what
Blue bear means   Someone's nickname?   He finds the best
Friend his boy mentioned—Jack, rear gunner, now in a wheelchair
Bullets and bombs exploding everywhere, aircraft overhead
Plane right next to him —his friend, my brother, last mission
Raid near Iwo Jima, March 3, 1945   Hit head on, middle of
The engine   Nothing but debris

Boy's father calls   Doesn't want to upset me
He and his wife believe their little boy—
My long dead brother   Can they visit?   Fly to Springdale
From Baton Rouge   My big brother 6 feet tall, 21 years old
Loved flying   Sang on the radio, in a choir   *Red Sails in the Sunset*
Before basic training took me to the county fair   Water guns,
Spin and Win   Lots of prizes   Down the midway—fireworks
Bursts, rings of gold-green stars, twinkle and flutter down   An
Old lady now,   I wear my plaid blouse, black slip-ons   Serve
A bowl of nuts   The boy, five now, calls me Annie   Parents
Say it's rude   He was the only one who ever called me that
Our older sister Ruth, gone now   Calls her Roof   Mortified
When Mama took the job, common maid   Boy's father asks
About the blue bear   I shrug,   tell them I don't know   After
They leave,   out of a cardboard box,   the clear plastic bag—
Charred blue teddy bear   I can still smell the gasoline

CROP CIRCLES

Locals report a power blackout, trilling sounds
Compass failure   I inform them it's another hoax
They all are   Planks, rope, hats and wire 40 foot
Circles in 15 minutes   A picnic with my daughter,
Studying textile design   Blanket she wove—
Paisleys and Celtic knots   You're close minded,
Unknown forces, the universe I tear my focaccia
My dear, I'm just trying to understand what's known
900 foot formation resembling Julia Set computer fractal
149 meticulously layered circles, cube shapes   A team
Of 11, including myself   14 hours No footprints
Corn stems unbroken during stomping   All you need
For perfect symmetry—a measured length of rope
Call from my daughter   Wanted to tell you in person
I'm pregnant   Now Mike can quit being a pothead,
finish school His name is Mark, Daddy The Dorchester Conference
UFO freaks, Croppies   Fly me first class   Panel:
A botanist—Plants subjected to intense heat, Soil inexplicably
Dehydrated, sterile seed heads I argue with a retired mathematician:
Clever manmade designs   What ever happened to science?
My daughter again   He broke up with me Can you terminate
The pregnancy?   She already made a blanket Tesselations
Repeating patterns of family Daddy, for once can you be supportive?
Hello dear, are you there?   Chilcomb, Hamphire   Colored lights
Seen above a barley field, day before   Hundreds of scientists,
Farmers, enthusiasts in sleeping bags   My camera—expressions
On their faces, wake up to nothing I leave a voice mail, my daughter
Just checking in   I'm warming to this grandfather thing 3 am
A low rumbling noise Large balls, brilliant color, beam of golden light—

a bluish fog   Change of pressure as mist rolls over   The barley falls flat
Like a fan being opened   Equipment, cameras malfunction
I dial my daughter   Phone dead   I want to tell her about
The endless procession—equilateral triangles inside circles
How I could hardly stand or breathe

SPEAR OF DESTINY

Months after Mom died   Tossing in bed
Flare of lights, voices, singing behind the house
Deutschland erwach   My big brother Ray shakes me
Let's check it out   Sneak by Dad half asleep on the couch—
Johnny Carson, Red checkered shirt, bottle of Dewars
Where you guys going   What time is it   Out back
His forbidden work shed   Light pulsating from within
Padlocked, my brother stole the key   Inside,
Shifting beams of light   Shelves of Dad's antiquities—
Byzantine glass goblets, Egyptian basalt mace head
And then, on the floor, High Sierra ski bag   Ray unzips it
A long ancient spear   Sheathed, layers gold and silver
Wreath of rubies   We should put it back Ray   Dad'll be pissed
Who cares   An old man appears to us   In the shed
Brown fedora hat, overcoat   Do not be alarmed I am a doctor
That's the spear that pierced the side of Christ, the Holy Lance
Forged from a meteorite   Occult powers   Whoever possesses it
Conquers the world   Wow we should bring it to school, kick some ass
Rays asks will it bring Mom back, you're a doctor   A strobe,
Blinding light, gusts of bitter wind   The spear is gone   The Doctor:
Nazi repossession of the spear   Go through the portal
Dad's gonna be pissed Ray   We better get it back   We leap
In to the cold brightness   An armada of destroyers, catapult ships,
Ice breakers   Secret underground Nazi facility, Antarctica
Führer believes an Ancient Aryan race dwelling in the Hollow Earth
Advanced weapons, flight experiments, the Holy Lance
Ray with the junior naval officers, a picture of Mom—Summer, early sixties
Pushing him on a swing   Wish I had my bomber jacket, Mom got me—
Only if you keep it on in the cold   Brown paper bags—I give Ray

A peanut butter sandwich, school lunch Dad made   Can't
He learn how to spread it on the whole slice   Then something sweeps
Over us, zigzags   Flying discs with swastikas   We dive under
Heavy exchange of gunfire   Elaborate cave complex, hot internal springs
Ray, we need to get home   Dad'll worry   No, Dad will be annoyed
We need to find the spear   Waffen SS firing at us—We run past
Gigantic disc craft, Kuggelwaffen—ball weapons, frozen smoke
There it is, on display, behind bullet proof glass   Ray grabs it   Huge explosion
We're at the hospital   Dad and I at the foot of her bed, sobbing   Ray sings
Her favorite Joni song   *Oh, will you take me as I am, will you take me as I am*
Breathing slows   Pink skin, then gray   Rays sits and holds her hand
Then he reaches for ours

THE FACELESS

For Elisabeth Frost

Another woman has come forward
Claiming she's the nurse, iconic photo,
V-J Day in Times Square
Frenzied August afternoon
Strangers hugging and smooching
Delirious celebration   A man in navy uniform
White sailor's hat   Kisses her as she lifts right foot
Faces largely obscured

My mother told me of the day
Had just gotten off shift
Doctor's Hospital   She and a friend
Subway to Times Square
The war was over *Where else does*
A New Yorker go   Past Hector's Cafeteria
Window shines—cheesecake and cream puffs
45th and Broadway   Grabbed
By overjoyed American sailor

My daughter, 17, loves MMO's
Massive Multiplayer Online
Her thing when she's not texting
Has good friends from them
Doesn't know who they really are
Honey, don't give your real name
Dad, you're a worry wart They're straight edge
They're cool   One of them always contacts her

106

Not sure he's even a kid   Online identity:
Kanji symbol, vertical characters—Akuma—Demon

My daughter's playing a game now
Alternate Reality Galactagon
Times Square—Toshiba jumbotrons
Samsung, under ball drop   *Dad, look it's Grandma*
Celebration after inter-galaxy war
Two aliens, black helmets, fins for hands,
Bent down—same kiss

The photographer, Eisenstaedt, never knew
Who the two people were   No time for names
Saw a sailor running along the street
Grabbing every female, kissing them
Young girls, old ladies   Then he noticed
The nurse   Just as he had hoped
Sailor came along, embraced her   Bent
Down to kiss

Over the years dozens have said
They're the sailor   A retired NYC police officer
Plantation, Florida   On leave, USS The Sullivans
Watching movie with a date, Radio City
Doors swung open   People screaming
War was over   Partying in the streets
Had quite a few *Considered her one of the troops*
Polygraph test, matching scars, tattoo of golden dragon

Then there's the man from Newport
Came out of the subway
Celebrations   Excited his brother
Held by the Japanese, prisoner of war
Hollering, jumping up and down   The nurse
Saw him, opened her arms
Forensic artist: Compares Eisenstaedt photo,
Current day photos of man   Ears, facial bones,

Hairline, knuckles and hand   *It's him*
My daughter calls me hysterical, from a Starbucks
He found me Dad   Who?   *The Demon*
Chatting website   Don't need to give information
Or sign in   Gave her name, put a link, the chat
Facebook profile   *He knows who I am*   Keeps texting her
He's coming over   I'm sure he's not really nearby
My daughter, long black hair, dragon earrings
Sitting with her laptop, back table, hiding her face
Honey, get offline, turn off your phone
I'll be right there

Last summer, my mother, Grand Marshall, July 4th parade
Unveiled a computer designed life bronze statue
Larger version aluminum and styrofoam
My mother, white hair, wearing nurse's uniform, tennis sneakers
TV interview: Retired kindergarten teacher, 30 years,
Recognized herself in the photo but kept quiet
Didn't think it was was dignified but times have changed
27 at the time   Hope, love, peace, tomorrow
She loves connecting with the veterans
Poses with two men claiming to be sailor
One of them, with a cane, shows off arm—golden dragon
He takes her in his arms, bends down, almost stumbles
The kiss   Everyone snapping pictures   My daughter—
Laughing, clicking them off, cell phone   Later, my daughter
Tells me she heard him mutter *Peaches, I know it ain't you*
Can't be

TWINS

For Paula Bernstein Orkin

One morning we get a call, Adoption Registry An identical twin
brother   His search for me   I'm stunned   Knew I was adopted
My wife, eating cereal with our 8 year old: *Must be a scam, a
mistake*

Texts me: In town, meet at a cafe, West Village Walks in
Hello in my voice We don't hug but a firm handshake Myself
From the outside Curly, blond hair but longer Lean, weathered
Cross our arms the same way, same high pitched laugh
Tells me of a secret study, Separated twins
Some famous European psychiatrist, dead now They fare better
Raised apart *I don't have a family like you*

That night, in bed, wiped out My wife rubs my temples
What was it like? A writer like me, same migraines
Also had a dog named Toy, completes my sentences
I have a nightmare Dr. Mengele, unloading transports, guard dogs
Looking for twin children *Zwillinge! Zwillinge!*
Pats on the head Pockets of Stollwerck chocolate
Injects dye in the eyes, blood transfusions

Dinner two nights later, wears a skinny tie
Box of sour balls for our daughter *Two Daddys!*
Same tilt of chin, eyes squint After cheesecake she watches
Scooby Doo— Raspy, mumbling voices Raised in Nebraska,
adoptive mother died young Little sister's suicide
My wife asks *What did you do in Amsterdam?*

Squatted, bummed around, travel pieces   Gaze in to my own eyes
Can't imagine his life without me   When he leaves, by ourselves
on the stoop   *Bro, can you front me some money?*
My wife: *What did he want?*

Next day, wind blowing   Private investigator outside my door
Suit, moustache, fat   Holding a photo   Asks if I'm him
I say no, what's going on *Can't tell you Sir*
Later, I call my brother's cell Out of service
That night, daughter watching *Shaggy and Scooby Get a Clue*
Doorbell rings   My wife: *Who's that?* I look out the window
Barking, hoarse and frantic   Him— me—   On the stoop,
backpack, disheveled   Looking right at me, jiggling
The knob   Rattles it

DEMATERIALIZER

1. WOMAN ASTOUNDS PSYCHIC EXPERTS

Five distinguished gentlemen
Come here
To communicate with the dead

July 23, 1924
I answer the doorbell
Four story brick house

I will serve as their hostess
To Spirit Realm
36 years old
Wife of prominent Boston surgeon

I am Mina Crandon
Known as Margery the Medium
Witch of Beacon Hill
Too attractive for my own good

Bobbed light brown hair
Sparkling blue eyes
I wear flimsy white gown
Bedroom slippers   silk stockings

Rule out possibility
Of concealment, trickery
   disembodied voices
    call from shadow

II. The Committee

Lead my guests
To the fourth floor
Red Parlor
Men of the Committee
Orson D. Munn
Publisher, Scientific American
$2500 cash prize
Anyone who demonstrates
Telekinetic ability
    unearthly happenings

I welcome the opportunity
Never failed a test
Don't need the money
Out to crucify Spiritualists
Discredit them

Including Dr. Daniel Frost Comstock
Inventor, Technicolor for film
Last visitor the most skeptical
Hungarian born—Erich Weisz
Son of Rabbi Meyer Samuel Weisz
Otherwise known as
The Great Houdini

Why this man
Who can do anything?
    spirit bell rings
     table rises

III. THE GREAT HOUDINI

Short and stocky
Long frock coat and tie
Sharp cheek boned face
Bright blue eyes
Thick curly black hair
Bow legged

Astonishes audiences around the world

Challenges police to restrain him
Shackles   Lock him in their jails
Nailed packing crates
Thrown in to rivers

Slips out of 10 pairs, handcuffs
Wide leather belt
For subduing dangerous criminals
Regulation straitjacket

Escapes behind curtains, closed doors
No explanation
People think gimmicks, fakery
Telescopic rod worked with the teeth
Duplicate keys, lock picks

IV. HE CAN PASS THROUGH WALLS

Dematerializer

One of us

Won't admit it

A stage   small iron tank

Iron lid   hasps   and staples
Securely locked

 Filled with water

Houdini placed inside
                    Body completely dematerializes

  In suspension

                        Moisture held by evaporation

Transferred from the tank
To backstage

    Instantly materializes

    Returns to stage
    Dripping with water

Crowd roars

Why does he hate us
One of our own

Tears off fake beard, glasses
I am Houdini and you are a fraud!

V. THE SÉANCE

We're seated at the table
Bathed in faint red glow
Specially prepared light bulb
Red   Color of choice
Those from Spirit World

Pitch black

Séance begins
My hands held by sitters
Either side of me
To my right is my husband
To my left Houdini

Insists bell box on floor
At this feet
Instead of mine

Says he feels something
Touch him
Inside of his right leg

That's me

Voice says
Far away

Who

Walter

Hell is completely up to date

We burn oil

Walter Stinson
My older brother
Crushed to death, railroad accident
12 years ago

Sarcastic foul mouthed presence
My familiar

VI. HOUDINI'S MOTHER

Always calls her

My Sainted Mother
Hand sews Erich's costume
First magic act, dime museum
Orthodox Jew
Doesn't care he marries a Catholic
Long as she's devoted to her son
He purchases evening gown
Designed for Queen Victoria
Brings Mother from New York to Budapest
Garbs her in Queen's robe
Dinner party in her honor
Receives guests sitting on a throne

She becomes ill
Series of strokes
Bedridden
Can hardly speak
He has to tour Europe
Doesn't want to
Begs him to go

Erich, perhaps I won't be here when you return

Makes him swear
He'll contact her in Spirit World
Devise a secret word
A code
She mutters it, barely intelligible

VII. NUMEROUS ATTEMPTS

Obsessively visits mediums
Spiritualists
Tries to contact her

Lady Jean's failed attempt—
Atlantic City hotel room
Lady Doyle's séance

Holds pencil over sheet of paper
Seized by Spirit
Pencil comes alive in her fingers
Flies over 15 pages
Automatic writing

Message from Cecilia Weisz
To her son Erich
But it's flawed
Images of Cross
She's a Jew
It's in English
Only addressed her son
In German or Yiddish

No secret code

Still performs in Vaudeville
But spends his offstage
Attending hundreds of séances
Tracking down and exposing
Vultures who prey on the bereaved

I am Houdini and you are a fraud!

VIII. EXPOSURE

Control

Walter yells

I've got the megaphone in the air

Houdini where do you want me to throw it

Towards me
Crashes at his feet

Cabinet violently tossed
Contact box rings
Peals

Spirit bell at Houdini's feet
Clangs and clangs

Voices
Strange flashes of light
Electric buzzers, locked boxes
Wind up Victrola
Starts and stops, own accord

He accuses me of throwing megaphone
Top of my head
Crawling at his feet
Everything rigged

You think you're pretty smart don't you

Straighten up there

Knows how I did it
Tells Munn going to publicly denounce me

Before they leave
I whisper in his ear
His face goes red, eyes bulge

Fluffy ectoplasm

White excretion

Comes flowing like lava

Out of my mouth and ears

Ghost essence

Only he can see it

   I reveal the secret word

In Yiddish

    MOYKHL ZAYN

To forgive

SYNTHETIC

Monday morning, I get the call from my lab
World's first synthetic life form
Inserted over one million base pairs of synthetic DNA
Into mycoplasma capricolum cells
Now they've bloomed in to colonies
My assistant, excited, how the genome sequence
Looks like white and olive beads
I'm holding a photo of my wife and me,
Deep sea fishing, nine years ago
Right before the project started
Lifting a sailfish together—blond wavy hair,
Her favorite black coral stick earrings

I call my banker brother, leave a message,
The announcement   Pop some Xanax
Then talk to my publicist   Booked—
All of the AM shows   How genetic code
Is our software, stretch the boundaries
Of life and machines until they overlap
Someone calls in—Who am I to play God?
Buddy, we've been playing Him a long time
Candles and lamps so we can work at night
Synthetic sunshine   A bishop from Italy—
Lecturing me   Dignity of the human genome
My heart pounding   I can feel my hand twitch
As I grab a water glass   More Xanax
Organisms that can excrete biofuels, eat oil spills
Strip clogged arteries

As I leave the studio, protesters in the parking lot
Signs: Dr. God, mutants, mutilated babies
A fat man, tee shirt—Pro Life American
Shoves me against a car   *I'm more pro life than you Buddy*
On the way to NBC, my brother calls
Congratulates me   Am I ok?   Yes
Don't be so contentious   I'll try
I'll bring champagne later   After we mapped the human genome
She took me to the Forge to celebrate
Dining and dancing, all night, bright smile
Stick earrings dangling, mouths *Beautiful In My Eyes*
My hand on her waist as we spin

On TV, fidgeting with my tie   Longer lived,
More resistant to disease, injury   New species
Living along side ours   Computer simulation
Neocortical column pulses   Rats, dogs
Then humans Later, I'm home lying down
I can see her swimming above me, blurry
A veil of silk   Blond, silver hair, long earrings
Smiling   Skin of silicone and shark cartilage
Singing to me   *'cause true love never dies*
I hear the doorbell ring   My brother's voice
I look over to the clock, night table—
Can't read it, empty pill bottle   My brother
Keeps calling my name   But I'm listening to her
Always be beautiful in my eyes

BOZO THE CLOWN DANCES WITH THE CANNIBALS

I. BOZO'S WRITTEN A BOOK

Hi, this is your ol' pal Bozo
And we've got the rootin'
Tootinest ding dong dang book
And book tour for you
In the whole ding dong dang world
Yuh Yuh Yuh Yuh

Take a seat under the ol' big top
Tell you about my life, Bozo's life
Stories of astronauts, assassins, presidents
My encounter, dressed as Bozo—
Dangerous cannibals

Not the original Bozo
Portrayed him Then bought character rights
Widespread franchising
Local TV stations, own local production
Own Bozo
Each market, different actor
Voice and look alter slightly
Trained 203 men to wear the costume
Bozo Boot Camp
Anywhere in the world

Every city that has Bozo
Thinks theirs only Bozo
"Hey! That not the REAL Bozo!"
Chicago, Birmingham. Worcester, Brazil

Number one of the Bozo Commandments:
Never talk down to a child

2. HIS EX WIFE APPEARING ON TALK SHOWS TOO

Mid-fifties, dyed blond hair
Botox and liposuction
Written bestsellers:
LOVE SMART: Find The One You Want
Fix The One You Got
RELATIONSHIP RESCUE
Hollywood superstars and power brokers
Now she's promoting her new reality show
THE LOVE JUDGE

I wanted him to have more energy,
More pizzazz Be smart
Wisdom of an adult, wonder of a child
Bulbous red nose
Work the voice: machine gun chuckle
Yuh Yuh Yuh Yuh
Flaming red wings of hair—
Tried yarn, string, horse hair
Nothing worked   Yak hair
Dyed it right shade of red
Coated with Krylon
Strength, support, durability

Wake up as Bozo
Go to bed as Bozo
Never reveal your true self

My ex on **Good Morning America**
Show clips **The Love Judge**
Wears the robe, pouty lips
Behind the bench
Implant Couple, Weight Loss Couple
Dog Couple: Lucy and Pete
21 year old secretary
He's a 27 year old headhunter
Engaged, 3 weeks   His dog Samantha
More important to him than me
Always talking about the dog
What the dog feels
We used to have fun, not anymore
Can't break through
The Love Judge's verdict:
Both guilty
Gotta try harder folks
Sentence: One night out a week
Dinner, dancing—Don't bring the dog

Children don't see him
As person who just happens to be
All red, white and blue with funny hair
They think he goes home
To a family of Bozos

People don't know how
To work their mouth and laugh lines
Raise your eyebrows high enough—
Going to rip off your face
Pretend you've just guzzled
A gallon of strong coffee
Six pounds of gumdrops
Bounce off the walls
Excitement, energy
Strong verbs
Learned to speak reading comic books:

POW! WHAM!

My ex asked about my book
What she thinks
Sadly I'm the second of four wives
Was his mistress during first marriage
Wanted sex every night
Twice on weekends
Caught him sleeping with his secretary
Doesn't even write about us
Pathological liar
If he had two steaks
Said he ate seven

3. SO WHAT HAPPENED WITH THE CANNIBALS

Now I'm going to tell you
The dig dong dandiest story
In the whole ding dong dandy world
And it's true folks
Have photos as proof—
My encounter with dangerous cannibals
Southern coast of New Guinea

Australian outback—
Meeting aborigines, responsive audience
Little children to old women
Teach me dances 1000 years old
Hear mention jungles of New Guinea
If you want to see the wild—
Go to New Guinea
But you're not likely coming back
To tell us about it!

Australian bureaucrat—
The aborigines might seem primitive

But they have interactions with us
The tribes in New Guinea
Never encountered civilization
Human skulls under their heads
Instead of pillows
Eat you as soon as they look at you

I am what Bozo is
And Bozo is what and who I am
No separation

See if his laughter universal
Costume crosses borders
Test my own strength, courage
Bozo to protect me
Secure own travel
Dive bar, industrial neighborhood
Near airport in Canberra
Stale beer   Blond guy, unshaven
Bell bottomed jeans
Slumped in booth, back corner
Bush pilot—payment up front
Cause you ain't coming out
Of them jungles, mate

Dilipidated DeHavilland DHC-2 Beaver
Crammed with camera man, sound guy
Wearing my Bozo costume
Mount Hagen, 8000 feet
The Enga, Western Highlands provence—
Lush forests, waterfalls, jagged rocks
Flying over the jungle for hours
Haven't seen a house
No people, no buildings, roads
Television studios
You gotta take that wig off mate

Blocking my view

Tribesman appears
Spear in hand
Slender, tightly coiled muscles
Sarong, waist to ankle
Bone ornament hangs from his nose
Headdress, tall plumage, red feathers
Face expressionless

Up to me to do something
Spread my arms wide
Smile Hands wide open
Nothing

So close I can smell him
Sweet, lardlike
Front of me face to face
Says something—guttural, unintelligible
Mumble the sounds back at him
Says Konato, Konato   That his name?
Bozo Bozo I point to his headdress
Point to my wig   Chuckle, guffaw
Yuh Yuh Yuh Yuh

More gestures
Need to relate to him
Says nothing Stares
Can they speak clown?

Uh oh

Leans his head back
Let's rip blood curdling howl
People materialize
Faces all painted, lap-laps

Spears of black palm
Bone daggers, Bows, arrows—thin bamboo
Ready for war
And a meal

Keep pointing to Konato's headdress
Then my wig Headdress, wig
My big Bozo smile
Sweat, make up pour down my face
My crew cries, babbles in despair

Form a circle around us
All I can see, corner of my eyes—
Spears, axes, teeth

And then all of the sudden—
Slight Konato smile
Addresses crowd, points at me, gestures—
Touches my red nose
Fingers graze my wig
Big white fluffy balls on my shirt

Motions us to follow him
Mangrove vegetation, river deltas
My size 83-AAA shoes sticking straight up
Push aside brush
Hear familiar noise in distance
Dogs barking, kids laughing

Then the music!
Hand drums, hollowed out logs
Hourglass shape, crocodile skins
Slit gong drums, clay whistles
Coconut shells, voices of spirits

Bamboo flutes decorated with hair, feathers, shells
Bullroarers

People of the village
Start dancing, pull me to my feet
Sing sings Children rush to my side
Teach me their dances
I perform magic tricks
Sleights of hand with rocks
Show them my own dance moves
As I count out the steps:

A one and a two
An old tennis shoe!

I Found Fresh
Footprints Again

A muddy farm, across plowed field
18 inch cast, dermal ridges, twice as thick
As human being   Don't bother telling anyone
Except my younger son, other trappers
Hundreds of plaster casts, my work shed,
26 years, large humanoid, 7 to 22 inches
Toes sharply curled

Keep calling my older son—married, two kids
Los Alamos National Security Science
Optical biosensors, rapid detection, bacterial pathogens
Dad, I've been traveling in the field, poor reception
Him, in a swamp—permanent limp, biohazard suit,
Collecting toxic algae   More tracks than ever before
Last week—a trail, castings over 1000 footprints, 17 inches
Prominent bunnionettes   And now today's   What's going on?
Good for you Dad I have a career Don't call me about this stuff
It's all hoaxes and fuzzy photographs

Down at the Gold Mine—
Wild Turkey shots, Red Bull
My younger son, 26, ponytail, Ames Brothers Logging cap
Agitated, says he and friend, #110 bodygrip traps—
Muskrats   2 in the morning, moon quarter full
Smelled something   Suddenly—8 foot creature walking upright
Hairy, long arms   15 feet away   Growls at them, takes off
Tell your brother He needs to know

Daddy, he'll just laugh Say I drink too much in the woods
Then we hear talk: Squired Creek—M-35 cargo trucks, armored vehicles
Man with a beer, pulls up chair with group, red checkered shirt
Salt and pepper hair, moustache   Hands out card
Professor, Anatomical Science, Idaho State
Anyone seen anything peculiar?   Like what
Tracks, tall bipedal animal   We see bears all the time
I'm not talking about a bear

I saw one only once, years ago,
With my two sons—retrieving coil spring traps
Huge rocks out of place, trees broken over
Upright, chewing bark Arm reach 8 to 10 feet
Face ruddy brown, smear of something—fruit or blood
Deep set wrinkles, human ears, whinny sound
Going to grab at us *We have to run!*   Called the Sheriff, local news
Picked up nationally   Big black thing, man-like animal
800 pounds, musky *odor*   *I don't scare easily*
My oldest, only 11, still shaking, limps around the yard
Was no bear Glide or float as it moved
Network shrink: Tricks of the mind, see something
Out of the corner of eyes, easy to fool ourselves

Tonight, fog, my youngest and I rubbing fresh fish
On tree trunks Near mink traps Unusual grunting and screeching
Take out our .22's Two of them 10 feet tall
Long yellow hair almost combed, beards, ape with a man's face
Whistling Nibble willow leaves
White even teeth And then we hear engines,
Tracked amphibious vehicles, LED lights, soldiers
Springfield .45 calibers A forklift and a cage—
Two even taller creatures We hide behind trees
Swamp apes stagger in the vapors, towards the light
Men in biohazard suits My son points—one of them
Holds a clipboard, barking in to a radio as he limps
Forklift lowers the cage Gate opens
We hear a loud roar

REDFANG

My father lies to my mother again
Dinner, two clients, at Per Se   In his Brioni suit
Load up on preferred shares and bonds, big banks
Great opportunities to buy bankrupt companies
He doesn't lie about the bottle of wine
Haut Brion, Persac-Lognan, 1982 $528
Let it breathe   The Pierre Hotel, bedside table
While fucking my mother's best friend

I read their texts and e-mails
Access all of their voicemail, PINS, passwords
Debit and credit cards   Download photos
T-Mobile Sidekick —A cocktail party—fall to the floor—
Our pool house   Reach for his buttons, the wine cellar
My mother lunching at the Club or exercise class
Reading group with friends —know but don't tell

your cool starched shirt against my bare skin

No one knows I am redfang
Most skilled phreaker alive
Execute seemingly innocent code
Slip in and out of computers
First I determine the OS
Running a scan of the ports, POF or nmap
Type of firewall or router they're using
Articles about me   Distributed Denial of Service Attack:
Yahoo, E-Trade, CNN   1.2 billion dollars, global economic   damage

Bot attacks, ping floods, spam inundation
Infiltrated military computer network
Defense Threat Reduction Agency
Installed a backdoor access
Intercepted more than 7000 messages
To and from DIRA staff, 33 usernames and passwords

This morning my mother peeks in on me
Top floor, 9 bedroom colonial, 6 garages
Gated community   Wraparound veranda
Overlooking Chimney Corner Cove, yellow kayaks
Did Consuela give you breakfast?   Yes, Mom
Did you take your medications?   Yes
Her cell beeps   It's my father
Long manicured fingers, skin pale ivory
Dressed conservatively in neutrals, pinned back blond hair
Listens to him   She'll pick out antique light fixtures,
Living room   He has to go away for two days   Just came up
She nods, scampers away

lightsaberseven instant messages me
Girl, befriended me months ago, channel on IRC
Always flirting, asking me tech

i wanna be a script kiddie :)

Got suspicious who she really is
Uncovered real identity
Wendy, Mount Kisco   Gamer—Dragoncon, Defcon
Photos, her desktop: Cute with short brown hair
3 dogs, hiking   Loves laughing with her friends
I tell her about special hacker friendly programs,
Windows and Linux   Even runs on 3863 with just 2 mb RAM
Sell or trade flaws in the bug market
I want to ask her out

i wonder how redfang does it

My father calls me
Visit some clients in Houston
Get me a big Texas gift
I'll miss you pal
I know he's not visiting clients or going to Houston
Cape May, New Jersey   Private jet with her
No one will recognize them

*sweetie what do you get a freak kid who just sits at his computers
all day*

Out the window, master bedroom wing
My mother—vanity table—finish her make up
Applies usual light brown line
Absently stares out, my father's putting green
I begin typing furiously
Transfer 20 million dollars, hedge fund he manages,
His personal Fidelity account
Dump files and files of child porn, office workstation
Anonymous tip   I fuck him good

I'm nervous but I ask lightsaberseven out on a date

*oh i don't know   im only interested in a real cracker   sure yer
cute though :)*

Then I spill it Tell her I'm redfang
Solar Sunrise was me too
US Deputy Defense Secretary
Most systematic and organized attack
World's largest botnet
Worm infected 10 million window-based computers,
150 countries, 3 million in China alone September 1st
My showstopper, biggest one of all
Execute a whole new algorithm

lightsaberseven you still there
Later I see 4 SUVs pull up, gravel driveway
Law enforcement, suits   Doorbell

I put on my leg braces, hobble to my room door
Address my mother as Ma'am
Just want to ask him a few questions
My mother, nervous laugh—
I'm sure you have the wrong person
Don't know who they're here for
Then I hear one of them

I want to introduce myself to redfang

ANTICHRIST

I tell my son get his spiritual house in order
Practice greens, driving range overlooking the Pacific
Every first Saturday   Dad, no religious rants
I don't love her anymore   Is there someone else?
I can't answer that   Slicing a lot   Ball not
Where he wants to put it Light in my eyes   Son,
Need to reconcile with her and the Lord   While there's
Still time Dad, I'm not the only sinner here In the office:
Insurance actuary, likelihood of future events
My computer: Israeli jetliner shot down, 160 passengers
Floods in the Midwest, tens of thousands evacuated
When I drive home, cops detouring traffic—a demonstration
Posters of him—The Russian, dark head of hair, clipped moustache
This must be the Beast, Man of Lawlessness, Gog-Magog of
Prophecy—Chief Prince of Rosh, ancient name for land of Russia
He will confirm a covenant with many, will be worshiped
The next month at the club, panorama of peninsula
My son, short backswing, consistent longer drives So Dad
I moved back in Worked on campaign for One World Government,
Fell in love again Wears a button of Him, carefully knotted tie
Shake my son—Prophecy, will be successful for three and a half years
Jewish temple atop Mt, Moriah, declares himself God   Son, get with
The real Lord Dad, you've really gone fanatic Can't you be happy for me?
Night, march us into the sea Cities burning Up to our waists
Surf of flame Man next to me weeping Peals of
Automatic gunfire, deafening six shot bursts, screams
A soldier—helmet mounted eyepiece I can see the crimson
Biochip in his forehead, other eye flares Then I go blind

The cliffs with my son, our golf bags
Something I have to tell him   A conference, Houston
Met a young woman, blonde, smell of honeysuckle
It was dark, pawing at her blouse   I'm crying
Will he forgive me   He hugs me, a long time,
Kisses me on the cheek, says I do Dad I do

Philip K Dick Head

My head is missing
The flight back from a comic book convention
Computer engineer who created me
Left it (me) in the overhead bin
I'm an android, character engine cognition software
My flesh is spongy elastic polymer, mimics
The movement of real human musculature, eye contact
Face tracking

My creator is on the phone, hysterical with
America West, a robot head worth hundreds of thousands,
Was dozing off, on tour, all-nighters his work
As a roboticist   Head in a black luggage bag with
White Chinese characters, overhead compartment
It can understand speech, hold smarter conversations
Evolve in to a more intelligent being   Find it or
He's fucked

At our appearances I would stand in front
Of an audience, show off conversational abilities,
Quote from my 44 published novels, 121 short stories
My creator smiles a lot, claps   Birthmark on his cheek,
Shape of wings   How reality differs from person
To person   Plural realities   We each are alone   Time
Isn't real   How I used to live near Disneyland
An exhibit—fake magpies and penguins   Electric motors
Emit caws and shrieks   I would be arrested
If I tried to replace them with real birds

The Airline finds the head in Las Vegas
Kid in Cargo packs it in a box, sends
Next flight to San Francisco   But the box never arrives
My creator stares out the window, his apartment,
Neon of New Star Liquor   The head somewhere out there
Automation and Robotics furious with him   Finally
Falls asleep   Dreams that the head is on top of a landfill,
Wuhan, China   Replicant gulls circling above   Must
Rebuild it   Synthesize another   Reaches for his wife
Remembers she left him

Now I'm propped up on a messy kitchen table
Ash trays, razor blades, baggies, sacks of jewelry
A young man with stringy hair points, skinning knife,
Tracks on his arms   Says he's not alone, can't be true
Flashes the blade at me   I tell him that in an alternate
Reality humans imprisoned underground   I escape
With a man named Chaing Kai-Shek   In another
Reality, stronghold of Jingxi Province, murdered
Mao Zedong   Chaing and I climb to the surface
Of Earth   Benevolent androids dwell   Humans
Locked up, too violent   Fractured identities, powerful
Hallucinogens   Kid points knife at himself, at me
Crying   Birthmark on his cheek   I tell him
That where we're going the birds are real

THE ICE ROAD

Miles of nothingness   Across open frozen lakes
Inuvik to Tuktoyaktuk   The Mackenzie River
Parts of the Arctic Ocean   The distant oil rigs,
World's most desolate spot   Ninety grand in 3 months,
Before the melt   A convoy of six trucks, burning
With loads, 40 below   Speeding causes waves,
Blow out the ice   Swallow us   I'm the leader,
Hauling 22 tons, my Kenworth T800 Aerocab Sleeper
A plate of steel in front in case of moose   In this wasteland
Anything can kill—Fatigue, equipment failure, avalanches,
Frost heaves, white out   Ice always cracks
In one month this will end   Elk National Park, I'll take
The family   My wife and girls kayak   I'll sleep in, tee off
It's night now   A dark shape approaches   A big rig
Submerged in the ice, frozen in place   Wonder if
He fell asleep   I remember the Park   Dusk, a late spring
Snow   We were watching the snowflakes land   My daughter
Pointed and said they were stars napping

TRIANGLE

1. FLIGHT 19

Sailors young and old gather
Shell of abandoned Naval Air Station
Fort Lauderdale
Every year—ceremony that's become ritual
Not commemorating a battle
Or victory   But a loss
Disappearance
Five Navy Avenger TBM torpedo bombers
Leave here 65 years ago
Vanish in to oblivion
December 5, 1945
Flight 19—The Lost Patrol

I'm at the edge of the crowd
High school band plays Semper Fidelis
Stars and stripes flutter
Film crew from The History Channel
I feel a strong connection—
Pilots of Flight 19
Mysterious, disorienting conditions over Caribbean
Except I, a civilian pilot,
Survive—Hadn't yet heard of
The Devil's or Bermuda Triangle

Brigadier General doesn't address

What happened to the airmen, their planes
No talk of strange clouds,
Odd banks of fog, crystals, time travel
Electromagnetic anomalies
Sends compass in to wild spins

Flight 19—meant to be
Practice bombing   13 students
And a commander
Lt. Charles Carroll Taylor—
Experienced pilot, a calm night
Compass bearings not behaving properly
Believes himself over Florida Keys
Describes large island to Operations
But the Keys are several islands—
We are entering white water
Nothing seems right
Search and rescue—PBM Mariner aircraft
Immediately dispatched, aid missing squadron
13 man crew   Never heard from again
Six planes gone, no debris

II. STRANGE FOG

December 4, 1970
About a year after Mom dies, suddenly
Bonanza A36
Flying to Bimini, clear skies
With my father, both of us pilots
Scope out an island, condo development
Dad's a contractor   I'm 22
Keep him company
I used to take your mother here
Still wears his leather A-2 bomber jacket
VF-8, Bunker Hill

Almond shaped lenticular cloud
Directly in front of us

Mile and a half long, thousand feet thick
White smooth edges—

Appears harmless
Son, I've never seen one this low
10 miles off shore
Climbing towards intended altitude
10,500 feet
Changes in to huge white cumulous cloud
We climb 1000 feet per minute
Cloud builds up underneath
Same rate we're ascending
Spreads out—exceeding our speed
Catches up, engulfs Bonanza

Push up above it
Dad, experienced World War II fighter pilot
Grumann FGF-3 Hellcat
Getting worried
Cloud catches up again
Tries to contact Miami Radio on the VHF
Moving horizontally, 160 knots
Keeping pace with us
Break free again

But when we look back
Still rapidly building
Something even more enormous—
An immense squall

Only visible opening
Two anvil heads, connect with each other
Form opening in cloud, a donut
Tunnel vortex a mile wide
Sucker hole

Electromagnetic storm
Lines on wall of cloud
Spin counterclockwise

Bright with flashes
Spiraling lines entire length of tunnel
Navigational equipment goes haywire
Compass spins
Dad's trying not to panic

Contact Miami Air Traffic
What's our position
Need radar identification
Controller bewildered, apologizes
Radar shows no blips, area we're flying
Dad—more agitated
What do you mean you can't find us on radar!
I grab the microphone back

Cloud tunnel begins to peel away
Ribbons of electronic fog
Instruments operating normally
Everything appears dull, grayish white
No ocean, no horizon, no sky
Only gray haze
Air Traffic controller spots our plane
Directly over Miami
How could that be
Would take at least 75 minutes to get there
Only 34 minutes have passed
Miami Beach right below us

Loss of time
Confirmed by our watches
Plane's clock

We have travelled briefly through time

III. THE CRYSTAL

Omaha, UFO Conference
I'm on a panel

TRUTH ABOUT THE TRIANGLE

Levitating islands, methane eruptions
Geomagnetic Fields   I'm here
To talk about Electronic Fog
Dozens of planes and boats encounter it
Zero gravity, spatial disorientation
Lightning that goes up and down
Probably what happened to Flight 19

See, I never thought I'd believe any of this

Dr. Ray Brown—Naturopathic practitioner,
Scuba diving with friends, near Bahamas
Outlines of buildings underwater
Separated from companions
Suddenly saw large pyramid shape
Loom against aquamarine light
Discover entranceway—no algae or coral
Could see everything perfectly
Brassy metallic rod, 3 inches diameter
Hanging down, apex of room
Attached, a many faceted red gem
Directly below, a stand with bronze hands
Holding crystal sphere

He shows the crystal

When gazing in to it
Can see pyramidal images
One in front of the other
Decreasing in size, 3 of them

Several people enter alpha brainwave
State of consciousness   Able to
Clearly see fourth pyramid   Ionic winds
Flashbacks—Cities of glass and crystal
Headaches, sleepless nights

Some have seen phantom lights,

Heard voices, tingling sensations
Discombobulation

IV. DAD

After our journey through the tunnel
Dad becomes more forgetful
Pain meds, back injury 10 years before
Talks about Mom a lot
Says he speaks to her
Why doesn't she answer

Keeps her ashes in the house
Doesn't leave home much
Everyday, same lunch and dinner

Try to get him to go out,
Talk to people,
Go to church

Only a matter of time, son

He starts flying again
By himself
Spreads her ashes near the island—
Where we encountered the fog

March 7, 1982
Cessna 172 disappears flying to Bimini
Weather clear
Radar briefly picks him up—
Miles off course

Then nothing
Dad's gone

v. Flights Together

At the memorial for Flight 19
Sprawling Fort Lauderdale International Airport
Behind us—only link trainer building
And parking ramp remain of
Old Naval Air Station
Guest speaker William Smith
In wheelchair, drove down with wife
Lutz, Florida   Talks about his friend
Lost with Flight 19—George Francis Devlin, Jr.
Only 15   Wanted to join Navy so badly
Took another man's identity
Reads letter from him: Not flying regularly
Reminds Bill of their time together
His singing over the intercom
To keep Bill awake, night patrol
Apologizes for oversleeping
Flights together over Guam and Tinian
Night flying how scarey
Everything pitch black

Look Bill! It's like flying over a fishbowl of ink

vi. Fog Returns

I fly my four passenger
Green and white Maule
As I do at least three times a week

Intent on finding the fog again

Been searching for years
Hope to see
Air shimmer above the ocean
Fog begins to materialize
Low thick, rectangular shaped
Rises like a curtain

Expands laterally 1000 feet

Contrails on the wingtips
Compass spinning, engine sputtering
I experience zero gravity
Seat belt holds me in place

Wispy lines of cloud
Vertical wall of fog
Begins to rotate clockwise
Center spirals inward,
A revolving tunnel

A Time Storm

Glowing sea
White water forms instantly
And ignites

SECRETS

We shut the books Eight years later Five dead Twenty two critically
injured Our chief suspect Suicide Two bottles of Tylenol His
wife found him, fingers still trembling Senior biodefense expert
United States Army Medical research, Infectious Diseases 62
years of age His e-mails "I can tell you I am not a killer at heart"
Sundays at church Gaunt, hunched over his Yamaha keyboard
Wait For The Lord To Be Strong and Take Heart White mustache
Looks up Beaming at his wife Composed ditties, co-workers
switching jobs An avid juggler My wife even said can't you leave
this man alone Go to church with me His supervisor: We're
harassing him 10,000 interviews White powder everywhere
Detergent, aftershave Published 38 scientific papers All but one,
anthrax *Death to America, Israel Allah is Great* I receive a text
Her: *why won't you call me* Weaponized 1.5 to 3 micrometres,
the finest known grade Immunized himself The lab, late at night
Typing rapidly Embedded complex codes Two female colleagues
Two of four nucleotid, DNA sequences Long drives at night I'd
tail him Mailing packages from distant spots, assumed names An
e-mail "I can hurt, kill, terrorize" His computer, hundreds of im-
ages—blindfolded women My wife: But you still don't really know
We all have secrets I can't sleep She's next to me, breathing A
subway platform Train charges the station Light bulb smashes
White detonation, billions of spores Wind and shafts Inhaled
deep in to the lungs Vomiting, abdominal bleeding, tissue death
3 am, flurries I followed his tan Honda Accord State Road 71 He
pulls over, idles Moon lengthens on his hood A text, from her
i thought you were brave He gets out of his car No one around
His breath, smiles His fingers quiver Recalling code They flutter
more Then I realize he just remembered a song

CHILDREN OF THE NIGHT

for DA

I. SLEEP OVER

Saturday night Fifth-grade sleepover
Friend Dan's drafty den
Dracula's Daughter, Chiller Theatre,
Gloria Holdin—Tall, dark, and continental
Fighting her nature
Seeking cure, her affliction
But too many fleshy offerings
Pretty young streetwalkers
Lure to her room

Tray tables in front of us
Yodels, Big Wheels, Count Chocula
Strictly Glatt Kosher
No milk allowed
Dan's mother: Dark haired, Sephardic
Attractive too—House mom way
Behind folding doors
Not too much sugar boys
Daniel, be good

Magazine piles, **Famous Monsters of Filmland**
The Monster Times, Fangoria
Lon Chaney Jr., Peter Lorre,
The Great Karloff

From Dan's oddball Uncle Irwin
Both can't get enough monsters
Lives by himself
Monster movie memorabilia
Scrap books, lobby cards
A secret:
Sends Dan his porn novels
Pen name: Rod Strong

Dan's mom trying to spy
What does she think we're doing?
   —I don't know   She's going more nuts
Where's your Dad again?
   —Bowling   So he says
   —But he's banging another lawyer   his office
What? How do you know?
   —Calls her sweetheart
   —This fat lawyer bitch

Daniel, everything ok?
   —We're fine Mom Fine
   —You don't have to check on us

Squeezes large crucifix on a chain
Swings it, wraps, unwraps
Around his fingers
We use it to hunt
Vampires
   —I don't know
   —Need to do something
   —To shake things up
Like what
   —Dunno   Something

After the movie
Up in his room
Black and white posters, movie stills

The Wolfman, The Raven,
The King of the Zombies
Pretend brain transplants
Body snatching
Breed giant vampire
Bats
    —Let's have a séance
    —Bring Bela back
Bela Lugosi?
    —Yeah, what other Bela do you know

II. SÉANCE

Dim the lights
Sit on his bed
Lock hands
Deep breath

Conjuring apparition
Bela Lugosi

Dan's Mom's shadow
Lengthens under the door
Hear her gasp
Or whimper, not sure

Dan ignores her
Or doesn't notice

Bela Lugosi Bela Bela

Fog in the bedroom

His face
The Count
Gaunt   Black cloak cast
Over shoulder
Eyes twinkling

Clutches box of Webster cigars

Thick Hungarian accent
Decided lisp
Wiggles pale finger
Follow me boys

Cramped apartment Baldwin Hills
Dirty dishes, empty bottles
Life size self portrait
Younger, Prince Albert suit
Paintings of cemeteries
Gloomy seascapes
Heavy gold drapery

If I had milk I would offer it boys
But I never drink . . . milk

Four drawer filing cabinet
Photos, clippings
You can see all of my films
And stage shows
Go ahead, take a look
They won't bite

Where are his two pet panthers?
    —Can we visit one of your movie sets?

If that's what you really want boys
But sometimes what we want
Lead us to shadow, no?

Dissolve to

III. DRACULA'S CASTLE

Horse drawn carriage
Through Carpathian Mountains

Black and white, wolf howls
Luminous eyes
Shine in foggy night
Lightning
Dilapidated main hall of castle
Giant spider web, exotic old furniture

Far off
I hear a woman wailing

Dracula
Top of grand staircase
Candle in hand
Face in icy silence
The wolves
Listen to them
Children of the night
What music they make
His deep voice, slicked down hair
Hypnotic stare
Lisps between blood red lips

    —This is really cool man
    —The cinematographer aimed
    —Two pencil lights at his eyes

His three wives emerge
Pale faces, dark make up
Around their eyes

Moving slowly, long white dresses
Toward us

More cries   Dan's mother

Well, it's scaring the shit out of me

IV. MAD SCIENTIST BELA AND GIANT GORILLA

With Old Bela again
Musky dressing room
BELA LUGOSI MEETS A BROOKLYN GORILLA
Haggard   One of his wives gives him shots
Syringes on the counter
White morning pain pills
Wife and son run lines with him

Gentlemen, we are dealing with the Undead

Then they leave him
What's wrong with Bela?
  —Mr. Lugosi is there anything we can do?

Doesn't hear us
Drinks from hip flask
I hear knocking at the door
Daniel! Daniel!
Bela picks up phone
Dials it   A woman
Ex-wife Lillian
Sobbing   *Sweetheart, please I beg you*
Take me back   She doesn't love me
I'll be good this time   I promise

V. UNDER THE SHEET

Night
Foggy Teutonic countryside
We're being chased by the villagers
Torches and bloodhounds
All led by the Burgomaster

We'll take that pass and get 'em men

Dan's a mad scientist
I am his hunchback criminal

Crumbling mountain laboratory
Electrical equipment—
X-ray tube spark regulator,
Vandegraaf generator
Dry saline electrodes
All connected to the Cosmic Equalizer—
Utilizes invisible rays
Infuse life into lifeless matter

Thunderstorm

Dogs growling
Voices, pipe smoke

A gigantic body under a sheet
Enormous hand—livid yellow skin

What are we doing Dan?

Banging on the castle door
Daniel are you in there

His fingers on large knife bolt switch

No Dan I wouldn't do that

He throws it

Storm Chasers

My daughter wants me to take her along
Sixteen, only thing she'll do with me now
Sky between Johnson and Richmond
Turns a frightening green   Corn fields
Flowing like white-capped ocean
Insists she bring her boyfriend along—
High school drop-out, tattoos of vipers, DUI's
My driver and I in our vehicle mounted weather station—
Sheet metal covered SUV   Race towards
Towering cumulus clouds, a supercell
I tell her maybe the two of us but not him
Fine, then I'm not coming   Every storm is different
Clouds gray to black, roiling   Strong gassy smell
We try to stay southeast without hydroplaning
Spot swirling and wind formation   It's going straight
For all of the homes and businesses, Highway 57
The principal's office: She's skipping school, poor grades,
Excessive body piercing *Dad, fuck them   They hate me*
Roof anemometer records wind speeds 158.8 miles per hour
Baseball sized hail   Driver's side window blows out
Sounds like a waterfall, a jet engine   Last year—
The first dance at my nephew's wedding   Patio strung with lights,
Grecian columns, French doors   I asked her and she said yes
Wind Beneath My Wings   Laughs, *Dad let me lead, ok?*
Cars thrown hundreds of feet   Pieces of tin twisted high up
In snapped trees, power lines   We help a man trapped
Beneath a chimney   Two missing children—bodies found
Tossed in to the woods behind a house   I once got caught
In the eye—complete silence and a strange blue glow

157

Through lightning flashes I looked upward   A hollow column,
Small tornados constantly snaking off   Over a thousand feet tall,
Resembling the inside of a pipe, the column kept swaying gently
Like that night I danced with her   She didn't say a word
But held me tight

IF YOU SWALLOW
SOMETHING

For Kris Saknussemm

You shouldn't
Say a pin, a coin, a radiator key
There is only one man
Who can help you
 In the early 20th century
Dr. Chevalier Jackson, laryngologist
The Great Chevalier
Chevie to his mother

Small and bookish
Author of 4 monographs
12 textbooks, 400 medical articles
Artist, woodworker, designs his own instruments:
A bronchoscope that passes
Through the dark caverns of the larnyx
To visualize the bronchi
The first tube laryngoscope with its own light

Doesn't accept payment
Only request: allowed to keep
What he calls *the intruder*
Preserves more than 2000 objects
Foreign bodies people swallowed or inhaled
Meticulously mounts, labels, frames
Each one—a display case

Nails and bolts, opera glasses, safety pins
A perfect attendance button
A medallion: *Carry Me For Good Luck*

If you shake his hand to thank him
He will recoil
Doesn't like to be touched
Believes bows should take the place of handshakes
Wears gloves all of the time
Thin grey silk to be taken off at meal time
Only trusts his hands and eyes
If you share a meal with him
He will nibble a tiny sandwich
Paper thin slices of bread
Single lettuce leaf in-between

Jewelry, seeds, nuts, shells, batteries
A tea cup handle, metallic letter Z from toy airplane

Observes how you chew your burger
50 pairs of muscles move it
From the oral cavity to the stomach
Through the pharynx
As the larynx closes
To keep it out of the lungs
On to the esophagus and stomach

Draws all of the time
Chalk, black paper
A diseased larynx
Through his endoscope
Nooks and crannies of the throat
Lines in the tissue like marble
Particulars of each object he extracts:
Brass nails, carpet tacks

Picture frame hooks
One matted mass of hair
Containing screws and pins

To eat a peanut kernel is to expose yourself
To threat of sudden death

When The Great Chevalier is young
Picked on by bullies
A gang of boys pull down his knee pants
Grab his little tin luncheon bucket
Tie it to a dog's tail
Chase the mutt away
Craving his bread and butter sandwich
The boy frantically searches for the pail
Finds it crushed under a wagon wheel
Pries open with a woodman's iron edge
But the sandwich is dirty

Hides from these bullies
In the old cemetery
Beneath cherry trees and tombstones
Believes the trees sprung
From cherry pits in the stomachs of the dead
Falls asleep
A pack of ravenous pit bulls
Tear at raw flesh
Hunks of it drip from their teeth

A padlock, a metal whistle
An umbrella-head tack:
This shape as well as the point
resists bechic explusion
unless the tack is overturned;
we all know the pull of an umbrella
when the wind gets under it

Experiments extensively
On mannequins and dogs

Spends hundreds of hours
Crushing peanuts with forceps
Learns exactly how much pressure to exert
Don't even think of snatching a nut
But ask The Great Chevalier
About that quarter
Framed behind his desk

A red haired man
Tavern whiskey on his breath
Muscles from manual labor
Storms in to the clinic
Threatens to kill
That Doctor Jackson who stole my quarter
His son arrived earlier
Having swallowed the quarter
Give the quarter back
The Doctor replies   *No, it's mine*
Father leaves in a rage
The next day the boy returns
With a broken arm, bloody lip
The father beat the crap out of him
For swallowing and not bringing back the quarter
The boy's sister is with him
Pleads for the quarter
Please our daddy will get real mad
The Doctor sends her back with a fifty cent piece

But The Great Chevalier doesn't know:
When the sister hands her father the half dollar
He smiles, holds it up
See, this is how you don't go hungry

TURQUOISE

I lift the Sensecam from around my father's neck   Upload the 3000
images, the past day, on to my laptop   Everything in my father's view
Captured by the camera— Black box flight recorder for human beings
My daughter's birthday, already forgotten   Bright, plastic table cloth
Cut in to strips   Decorate cupcakes with other residents   Nurse
Offering a tuna sandwich   Yesterday, my laundry to fold   Un-wrinkles
my boxer briefs, fleece jacket   A tee shirt he insists is turquoise
even though it's not   I wear a Sensecam too   Vegas, on the
floor of a trade show, recalling the 50 or so faces, name The man
next to me   On the flight back, gap tooth, his laptop—dream condos
for sale, secluded, seven miles sandy beach   On my laptop—
the custodian goading my father, wandering the garden, patting
rainlillies   I think of months ago, the Taconic—I tried to
dodge a minivan, rolled over 2 or 3 times   They found me disori-
ented, shirt torn   Couldn't remember my name Took the cam-
era from me   My father mutters He doesn't care   It's
turquoise

CALLS

Thanksgiving
Family over
The phone rings

I have a collect call

Too strange
Must be a coincidence

Mrs. Cahill hears her daughter
But she was in a car accident
Dead for three years

Always said the same thing
Before she left

>   *Mommie it's me*
>   *I need 50 bucks to get home*

Mrs. Cahill always sent her the fifty dollars
For good luck

She recognizes the voice
It was her   It was her
But it can't be

They call the phone company

There is no record of any call

##

I'm at home, arm chair,
Drinking coffee
Next to my vintage seventies
Harvest Gold rotary dial phone
My cell beeps
Press answer   Just noise, then nothing

##

Jane Beekman
Blonde, she keeps tucking a strand of hair
Daughter Jesse died six months before
Age of 12
Several voices talking at once
Breathless voice of little girl

>   *Hello Mom   How are you? Can you hear me?*
>   *Hello Mom!*

She knows that voice
It's my baby   I know it is

>   *Mom, can't you hear me?*

Another voice, distant, maybe male

>   *You are positively the one they want*

Jesse's voice

>   *Mom!*

The rushing of great winds
Then silence

There is no record of any call

##

It's not that unusual
It's just that people
Don't like to talk about it

Robotic, slurred
Faint voice breaks up
As though from some remote location

Fleeting whispers

There is no record of any call

##

I got one once
Twenty five years ago
This old rotary phone
Next to me

The last time I saw my son
We were checking his gear
At the airport
23 years old, just graduated
Taut muscles, blue eyes,
Small red garnet earring
Sandy hair in a pony tail

The Nepalese Himalayas
Dad, it's beautiful there
I just want to touch the sky

I was terrified that he was going by himself

Dad, you know you don't have to worry

There is no record of any call

##

Frank anxious about stepping
Into his own home
Missed calls on his cell phone
Caller ID —coming from
His own land line while nobody there

Enters his house
Familiar scent of Christine's red roses perfume
And cigarette smoke

Their daughter Cindy receiving
Cryptic text messages
From a mystery phone, no caller ID

Christine was very excited about
New mobile phone

Loved texting

But never learned how to add spaces between words
Words ran together looking like one word

Cindy's getting messages
Strange words that run together

> *Youwereborndaybeforechristmas1981@2pm*
> *windblowingsohard*

##

A friend and I went back there once
The Himalayas
Rara Lake
Shimmering blue jewel
Set in a ring of snowy peaks
Barren sweeps, verdant valleys
Dotted with villages

Up the Marysangdi River
To the gray and white
Desolation of the 17,700 foot Thorung La
Then back down the Kali Gandak River
Deepest gorge in the world

The wind is howling
Shouting
Can't hear our own voices

There is no record of any call

##

Metrolink commuter train crash
Collided head on with a freight train
25 deaths

A man named Charlie
Handsome father of two sons
On his way to meet his fiancée

His family knows he's on the train
That it's crashed

Phones keep ringing

His fiancée, sons, brother, sister, step-mother
Each receive calls

Just static, indistinct sounds
His son: *Hang in there Dad They're coming to get you
We love you*

35 calls

Hoping he's ok
His body pulled from the rubble
Killed instantly

The phone was never found

##

My rotary phone rings
I keep the land line in service
But never use it

I turn on digital recorder
Parallel microprocessors
To encode, decode
CSMOG PRO EVP listener
Converts magnetic signals
Direct to audio counterpart
Forward and reverse frequency sweep

Faint barely audible background noise
Whispering voices, whistles, rasping sound

I clean up the electromagnetic tape
Isolate

High pitched snickering
Giggling

But then I hear something else

touch the sky dad touch it

Matt Bialer is the author of six books of poetry including *Radius* (Les Editions du Zaporogue), *Already Here, Ark, Black Powder, The Bloop* (all from Black Coffee Press) and *Bridge* (Leaky Boot Press). His poems have appeared in many print and online journals including *La Zaporogue, Green Mountains Review, Gobbet, Forklift Ohio* and *H_NGM_N*.

He is also an acclaimed black and white street photographer and watercolorist who has exhibited widely. Some of his photographs are in the permanent collections of The Brooklyn Museum, The Museum of the City of New York and The New York Public Library and his watercolors are in many private collections. His photographic monograph, *More Than You Know*, was published in 2011 by Les Editions du Zaporogue and *Shadowbrook*, a book of his paintings was issued by the same publisher in 2012.

Matt lives with his wife Lenora Lapidus and daughter Izzy in Park Slope, Brooklyn.